# COTTAGE
## *Retreats*

# COTTAGE *Retreats*

## Decorating Ideas for Every Mood

Lisa Jill Schlang

FRIEDMAN/FAIRFAX

A FRIEDMAN/FAIRFAX BOOK

© 2002 by Michael Friedman Publishing Group, Inc.

Please visit our website: www.metrobooks.com

Library of Congress Cataloging-in-Publication Data

Schlang, Lisa Jill.
    Cottage retreats: decorating ideas for every mood / Lisa Jill Schlang.
       p. cm.
    ISBN 1-58663-306-6
    1. Interior decoration. 2. Decoration and ornament, Rustic. 3. Cottages. I. Title.

NK2195.R87 S36 2002
747--dc21

Editor: Hallie Einhorn
Art Director: Kevin Ullrich
Designer: Lynne Yeamans
Photography Editor: Kathleen Wolfe
Production Manager: Michael Vagnetti

Color separations by Radstock Repro
Printed in U. S. A.

10 9 8 7 6 5 4 3 2 1

Distributed by Sterling Publishing Company, Inc.
387 Park Avenue South
New York, NY 10016
Distributed in Canada by Sterling Publishing
Canadian Manda Group
One Atlantic Avenue, Suite 105
Toronto, Ontario, Canada M6K 3E7
Distributed in Australia by
Capricorn Link (Australia) Pty, Ltd.
P.O. Box 704, Windsor, NSW 2756 Australia

*To my fiancé Matthew Siglag,*
*You are the sunshine of my life.*


*Special thanks to my editor Hallie Einhorn. Mom, Dad,*
*Julie, Eric, and all my friends (you know who you are),*
*I couldn't have done this without your love and support.*

# Contents

# Introduction

*opposite:* Whether poised by the sea or nestled in the mountains, a cottage serves as the ultimate getaway. Here, double-hung windows allow cool breezes to waft through a sitting area while providing a breathtaking vista of the ocean. To ensure an unobstructed view, the lower portion of each window is left free of mullions. Simple wood floors and white wicker furnishings contribute to the relaxed atmosphere. The result: a perfect retreat.

Cool breezes streaming through open windows, wind chimes ringing gently on the porch, beloved treasures infusing interiors with warmth and personality—these are the delights that make our senses tingle. These are also some of the charming and welcoming elements that make up the perfect cottage retreat.

Regardless of the particular location and style—whether a quaint shingled saltbox by the sea or a rustic log cabin in the woods—a cottage offers sheer enjoyment and relaxation. It is a place where you can unwind, a haven where you can get away from it all, even if only for a few days. It is a setting in which you are free to indulge in life's simple pleasures. For some, this means sitting back in a rocking chair on the front porch and soaking in the sounds and sights of nature; for others, it means escaping to the only spot where there is enough peace and quiet to read a book from cover to cover.

A cottage can also serve as a family retreat—a setting for playing catch in the backyard or enjoying hours of conversation over a savory home-cooked meal. During the summers, alfresco dining may be a daily treat, while the winters may call for gathering around the fireplace. But whether your cottage promotes quiet contemplation or buzzes with activity, it will certainly be a special place that provides plenty of memories for you and your loved ones.

## cottages: then and now

While today's cottages are cherished as refreshing sanctuaries—places that foster relaxation and rejuvenation—these structures were originally built for a much more fundamental purpose: providing basic shelter. In Europe during the Middle Ages, small cottages were were constructed to house serfs. While the reigning class lived in sprawling castles, the laborers resided in much simpler homes. Made from a timber framework topped by a high-pitched thatched roof, the cottage at that time was a single-story structure that generally had two rooms. One space held the hearth, while the other was a chamber for sleeping. Initially, the chamber was used by women only.

From about the mid-sixteenth to the mid-seventeenth century, cottages flourished in England. These diminutive abodes evolved from unadorned one-story homes to picturesque dwellings that often included a second level. They became prevalent in the countryside for both servants and farmers.

These structures offered an inherent charm that grew out of a need for affordable housing. Constructed from available indigenous materials, they seemed to be inextricably connected to the land. Roofs were made of such materials as slate, stone, and tile. Since glass was costly, early cottages had very few windows, and those windows that did exist were small, making these structures appear even cozier. Windows featured diamond-shaped panes divided by twigs—and later by lead.

When British colonists came to America, they built houses that emulated the characteristics of the European cottage. And by the early 1800s, settlers in Massachusetts designed a cottage style of their very own: the Cape Cod. The now ubiquitous structure included a gable roof and a massive hearth.

*opposite:* This spacious bath has a peaceful quality, thanks to a primarily white palette and a restrained use of accessories. The presence of wood warms up the space, while tongue-and-groove paneling around the tub and sink offer additional texture. A tall cupboard that holds its own against the soaring ceiling keeps towels and bath supplies conveniently on hand.

Another period of note in the history of cottages came during the mid 1800s. Although it was a time of increased wealth during which many grand homes with elegant Regency-style details sprouted up, people yearned for simplicity in their lives. The Romantic Movement—with writers like Edgar Allan Poe, John Keats, and William Wordsworth providing delightful descriptions of charmed places—had a strong influence on architecture. And wealthy homeowners were soon demanding second residences to serve as getaways. Then, in 1842, America's pioneer cottage designer, Andrew Jackson Downing, published a book entitled *Victorian Cottage Residences.* The volume popularized the Gothic Revival style and reinforced the architectural importance of cottages.

Today, cottages come in all different sizes and shapes and can be found all over the world. While the location of a cottage may dictate the design, as is the case with the saltboxes and Cape Cods of New England and the Victorian-style homes on the New Jersey shore, certain commonalities exist that transcend time and place. Regardless of the particular style, there is an overall simplicity, which most likely stems from the cottage's modest size and humble beginnings. Moreover, the materials used continue to be indigenous to the area in most cases. Mountain retreats tend to be made of logs from a nearby forest, while lakeside dwellings often feature stones found on the surrounding land.

Another shared trait can be found inside: a pleasing mix of furnishings. Pieces handed down from previous generations, flea-market finds, and collections from travels often make their mark on the eclectic scheme. An old-fashioned rocking chair may intermingle with a sofa that has gained new life from a loose-fitting slipcover. A collection of vintage blue glass bottles may be a nice counterpoint to a Zen-like contemporary kitchen outfitted with sleek stainless steel appliances.

The simple style, medley of furnishings, and prevalence of indigenous materials give a richness to these abodes. And this richness is deepened when you bring your own tastes and prized possessions to the mix. The unique details, after all, are what make a house a home.

## in the mood

Despite their underlying similarities, cottages can take on a variety of moods. While one person may favor a breezy seaside cottage outfitted with airy white wicker furniture and a soothing blue-and-white palette, another may be drawn to a cozy countryside dwelling filled to overflowing with comfy seating, layers and layers of textiles, and a happy jumble of collectibles. Still others may prefer a humble log cabin nestled in the mountains, complete with rough-hewn furnishings and camp memorabilia, while for some, a romantic hideaway that brings the feel of an English country garden indoors is the only way to go. In this book, we'll examine six different cottage moods—tranquil, romantic, cozy, nostalgic, rustic, and whimsical—and explore ways that you can achieve the effect you desire in your own retreat.

Whether you opt for floral patterns and lacy sheers or Windsor chairs and checked table linens, the individual flair of your retreat will come from the personal stamp you give it. And nothing is set in stone. The character of your cottage will evolve over time as you add new treasures and experience new things; in other words, your spaces will grow with you—and taking part in this progression is, indeed, one of the true joys of cottage living.

# chapter one

# Tranquil

IT'S IRONIC THAT WITH ALL OF THE ADVANCES IN TECHNOLOGY, INSTEAD OF MAKING OUR LIVES EASIER, WE'VE ACTUALLY

MADE OUR DAILY ACTIVITIES MORE COMPLEX. FROM CELL PHONES TO E-MAIL, WE ARE CONSTANTLY IN TOUCH WITH THE OUTSIDE

WORLD. EVEN OUR CHILDREN ARE INUNDATED WITH STIMULI—THE INTERNET, PAGERS, TELEVISIONS IN OUR CARS—THINGS WE

DID NOT HAVE WHEN WE WERE GROWING UP. OFTENTIMES WE YEARN FOR A SIMPLER WAY OF LIFE. WE YEARN FOR A PLACE

WHERE WE CAN SIT BACK AND RELAX—A PLACE OF TRANQUILLITY.

*page 12:* It's almost as if this home emerged naturally from the boulders. The seamless integration of architecture and site establishes a Zen-like effect. *page 13:* Situated just beyond the screened door of a quaint shingled cottage, a white rocking chair invites occupants to take a break and enjoy the outdoors. A wood bench provides additional seating, and a lantern-style fixture stands ready to shed light on the patio when the sun goes down. This is certainly a place for quiet moments and peaceful reflection. *opposite:* With its weathered shingles and blue-gray trim, this cottage is perfectly at home in its seaside location.

## a place of your own

Nothing promotes an air of tranquillity like a cottage by the sea. From charming Cape Cods with their weathered shingles and white trim to New England saltboxes with their crisp lines and tailored design, there are a variety of simply styled retreats that serve as peaceful escapes from the everyday world. Providing spectacular ocean views and ushering in cool sea breezes, these unassuming structures seem to whisk us away from the hassles of daily life and make our troubles melt away.

It is not necessary to live by the beach, though, to achieve a sense of serenity. Like a basic Cape Cod, any type of architecture that is simple in form and free of ornate details will help to set a tranquil tone.

Retreats that take their cues from Asia and follow the principles of Zen Buddhism, for instance, offer peaceful settings for relaxation. Designed to be free of distractions and to maintain a connection with nature, Zen-like structures feature clean lines and natural materials—attributes that are soothing to both the eye and the soul. Picture a naturally stained wood dwelling with a sheltering hipped roof and lots of glass windows that invite the outdoors in. Blending in with the surrounding landscape, such a retreat projects a calming sense of harmony.

## looking in

Inside the cottage, the layout of space can have an effect on the overall mood. Open-plan designs, where rooms flow freely into one another, suggest an ease of mobility and a sense of continuity from one area to the next. This setup, in turn, will affect the inhabitants' daily activities. The removal of walls fosters a sense of togetherness, allowing people in different areas to interact easily with one another. This aspect is especially helpful when entertaining. If the kitchen looks out onto the living room, guests can lounge comfortably while visiting with the host as he or she prepares the meal.

*opposite:* When privacy is not an issue, you can include plenty of windows to take advantage of the outdoor scenery. This beach house is enveloped in windows to provide sweeping panoramic views. Once inside, rooms offer an open and airy quality.

*right:* An open-plan design allows for easy movement from one "room" to the next while setting a casual tone. In this renovated boathouse, high ceilings, white-painted walls, and wood floors form the perfect backdrop for a delightful mix of furnishings. A ceiling fan not only adds style, but helps keep the space cool during the summer months. Crisp blue-and-white striped couches mingle with a red-and white checked throw and a jaunty, patterned tablecloth.

opposite: Tilt-out windows on two sides of this living space let ocean breezes in while shielding the space from moisture. Free of curtains or shades, the windows maintain the clean look of their surroundings. *left:* When the goal is a serene setting, less is definitely more. Bare floors, unadorned windows, and a minimal number of accessories result in a tranquil milieu. The use of natural materials, such as wood, affords these simple spaces a degree of warmth.

Similarly, such a design allows parents to keep an eye on young children playing in an adjacent space.

The backdrop of your cottage interior will also contribute to the feeling that pervades the space. Walls, floors, and windows all require consideration. To promote a serene quality, create a clean look by keeping floors and walls unadorned. If you feel the need for a little cushioning underfoot, try a sisal rug, as its neutral hue will fade quietly into the background. Plus, sisals—along with other tightly woven rugs—are low-maintenance in nature, as they can easily be shaken out to keep them clean.

When it comes to windows, consider forgoing drapes and blinds and leaving these portals to the natural environment bare. Open views bring the outdoors in, allowing occupants to reap the benefits of the landscape while enjoying the comforts of home. Imagine yourself relaxing in your living room as you savor your beachfront location. And what better way to enhance time spent cooking in the kitchen than with an unobstructed view of the outdoor scenery?

In places where privacy may be an issue, such as the bedroom or the bath, consider an architectural solution such as shutters—these can be left open when they're not needed. Whether stained or painted, wood shutters contribute to a tranquil ambience with their unpretentious form and straightforward geometry. Blinds are another suitable option. Slender wood blinds lend a streamlined look, while honeycomb fabric blinds offer a softer effect. For a breezier sensation, curtains can help create a light and airy atmosphere.

## COLOR TIPS

Before purchasing a few gallons of paint, make sure that you like the color. Most home centers will have smaller containers of the various colors so that you can try them in your own home. Paint a square that is at least 2 x 2 feet (60 x 60cm) on your wall. See how you like the hue at different times of day. The color will change its appearance as the sunlight goes in and out of your space. Also, examine how the color works with the artificial light in the room. Florescent lighting, for example, often gives hues a greenish cast, while incandescent bulbs may make a color appear more yellow. To create the most serene interiors, find colors that don't vibrate; instead, the hues should soothe the soul with their light, airy quality. Remember that the painted walls will be just a backdrop to what goes inside.

Picture gauzy white sheers floating gently in front of a bedroom window with white trim. If you opt for curtains, make sure that they have a tailored design. Layers of draperies are not appropriate for a peaceful sensibility. Remember that serenity is achieved through simplicity.

As you examine the backdrop of your rooms, think about how colors can affect your mood. Cool hues, such as blues and certain greens, will infuse a space with a restful effect. Imagine the walls of a bedroom bathed in a subtle seafoam or celadon. Or what about a living room decked out in a refreshing palette of blue and white—a favorite color scheme for seaside cottages? If you prefer something a little warmer—perhaps for a dining or living area—consider a pale yellow to create the effect of washing the interior with sunlight. White walls, of course, will give the most pared-down look. To achieve a bit more warmth than white, you can call upon neutral hues, such as beiges or taupes. But with neutrals, take care not to select a hue that is muddy.

## *easy living*

To ensure a tranquil environment, select furnishings that are low-maintenance. Why worry about fine furniture and delicate fabrics in a place that is supposed to help you get away from the daily hassles of life? Include durable pieces that will stand up to heavy use. For example, in your living room, consider Shaker-style tables and Mission sofas; not only are these wood furnishings sturdy in construction, but their clean lines speak to simplicity. For cushions, select fabrics that will wear well—ones that are easy to clean and won't pill. Consider applying Scotchgard to fabrics so that spills will be repelled. Patterned fabrics, like ticking stripes, or textural multicolored weaves will hide stains and soil.

Slipcovered furnishings are a good choice for achieving a low-maintenance interior. Available in a variety of shapes, styles, and sizes, loose-fitting slipcovers offer plenty of versatility while imbuing a cottage with a laid-back feel. You can either buy couches and chairs that come complete with slipcovers or place slipcovers over pieces you already own. Masters of the cover-up, these helpful devices are a great means for revitalizing furnishings that are worn—ones that have good bones but need new upholstery. You can take measurements and have a slipcover custom-made, or you can purchase an unfitted slipcover. The latter is made to fit over any style and can be found at retail bedding stores. The best part is that if a slipcover becomes soiled, you can just take it off and throw it in the wash. (Make sure to check the label before purchasing, as some slipcovers do require dry cleaning.)

As if all the aforementioned benefits weren't enough, slipcovers also allow you to change the look of your room relatively easily. If you get tired of a certain pattern or want to update the look of your space, simply purchase new slipcovers—this solution will be much less costly than replacing an entire sofa or set of chairs.

While certain furnishings promote a serene ambience because of their practical traits, others suggest an ease of living thanks to their style. Rattan, for instance, evokes the tranquil feeling of the islands, where warm breezes and turquoise waters lull the body into relaxation. Wicker, too, with its airy design and casual demeanor, suggests a carefree setting. When set against white walls, white wicker furnishings almost disappear into the background. While these pieces are great in a living room—picture a set of creamy beige wicker chairs around a matching table—they also work well in the bedroom. A small white wicker chair, outfitted

with a comfy seat cushion and positioned by a window, may be just the spot for early-morning coffee or late-afternoon reading. Highly versatile, wicker will help make your outdoor living spaces as delightful as your indoor ones—just make sure to use the weather-resistant variety.

## indoor pleasures

As you decorate your cottage, let the location and architecture dictate the style of furnishings and accessories. If you have a contemporary retreat with an Asian flavor, for instance, include streamlined, modern furnishings to give your haven a sleek appearance. In the living room, you

*opposite:* Sheathed in white and free of clutter, this enclosed porch offers a peaceful setting for reading and reflection. A white wicker chaise suits the airy surroundings, while a humble side table adds a bit of charm with its chipped paint. Nature becomes part of the decor, thanks to the abundance of windows.
*above:* In this Asian-inspired home, the clean lines of the modern furnishings echo the sleek silhouette of the contemporary architecture. A white paper lantern provides a fitting accent.

sun's changing rays will create various reflections and remind family and friends of the soothing quality of the sea. For the bedroom, try placing a tall cylindrical vase on the night-stand, and fill it with shells that you've collected during long walks on the beach. In a continuation of the theme, line up starfish on the top of your bathroom wall to create a crown molding of these ocean creatures. The inherent relaxing con-notations of water will fill your rooms with a peaceful air. Whatever the style you choose, make sure to keep rooms simple—almost shipshape.

To maintain a serene effect, try not to overstuff your cot-tage with too many sofas and chairs. If you need additional seating, opt for the built-in variety, which offers a pared-down demeanor. You can design a wood or concrete slab to cantilever from the wall and then place cushions on top. However, steer clear of too many loose pillows and throws because they will take away from your streamlined look. As for artwork, make sure the pieces you choose reinforce the relaxed setting. Black-and-white photography placed in a simple wood frame provides a calming effect; Japanese prints and watercolors of seascapes also offer a soothing quality.

## *pared down to perfection*

Setting a tranquil tone is easier than actually maintaining it. The key is to keep clutter at bay. Toward that end, you'll need to pare down. Take inventory of what you have, then eliminate what you don't absolutely need. Your great-aunt's collection of vintage rag dolls, for example, may not be appropriate if you are trying to attain a serene space. As you take stock of your possessions, one good rule of thumb to follow is to ask yourself if you've used a certain item over the past year. If you haven't, then it's time to get rid of it.

*above:* In a compact bath, a flowering branch delicately painted on the wall provides a decorative touch without eating up valuable space. Sprigs of real lavender release their calming scent into the air. *opposite:* Dressed in white and accented with blue, this kitchen has a pared-down look. Eurostyle cabinetry, devoid of detail, provides a streamlined appearance and much-needed storage, while Shaker-style bar stools offer simply styled perches at the counter.

might include a simple boxy white sofa with exposed legs flanked by armless high-style chairs, such as Mies van der Rohe's Barcelona chairs. In the dining room, you could introduce a wood table set beneath a paper lantern. For the bath, consider a Japanese soaking tub and an above-the-counter sink, where the basin simply sits on the surface.

If the architecture of your home leans more toward the traditional—a shingled beach cottage, perhaps—you will most likely take a different approach to achieving a tranquil mood. Popular for seaside cottages is a nautical theme. Set blue-and-white cushions atop white wicker furnishings to give your living room a crisp, clean look. In the kitchen, place a collection of sea glass on the windowsill so that the

*opposite:* Turn your bath into a sybaritic retreat. Here, a tub is placed beneath two small windows, so that the occupant can enjoy nature while bathing. An old-fashioned faucet, thick window trim, and painted paneling give the space its appeal, while the minimalist decor results in a serene effect. Aromatic candles make bathing a multisensory experience.

*right:* Subtle details—including a bouquet of white flowers and pillow shams adorned with shells—add personal style to this bedroom without being distracting. A canopy bed outfitted with sheers and a white coverlet creates a peaceful setting in which to drift off to sleep.

*left:* Pared down does not mean empty. As you can see, a tranquil bathroom may be enhanced with simple touches such as seashells, flowers, and even a colorful towel. The colors you choose also play an important role—here, the pale blue is complemented by the orange tones.

# STORAGE TIPS

*Out of sight, out of mind. Rid your spaces of any excess clutter to create a soothing atmosphere. In order to achieve this peaceful state, you'll need plenty of storage. Cottages, which are inherently small, offer more challenges than larger homes, so here are a few tips.*

*right:* You will rest easy when your interiors are kept simple. This bedroom is outfitted with built-in storage space—shelves and drawers—so clutter can be contained in an orderly fashion. A peaked ceiling, plenty of windows, and wood floors further promote an air of tranquillity, while a wicker rocking chair and a bouquet of sunflowers finish off the look.

🌿 **PLAN AHEAD.** If you're engaged in a remodeling job or a new construction, make sure to include storage space in your design. Take this opportunity to get the most out of your cottage. Design closets with built-in shelves and organizational aids such as cubbies, shoe ledges, and clear-front cabinets. Think about creating built-in benches or window seats that provide storage beneath the seats, as this extra space will help you to keep living areas and bedrooms looking tidy. Leaving surfaces clear of excess knickknacks will help promote a tranquil mood.

🌿 **BE CREATIVE.** If you think you don't have room for a linen or broom closet, think again; all you need is a little space between two wall studs to create ample storage (the space beneath a stairwell is a frequently overlooked spot).

🌿 **LOOK UP, LOOK DOWN.** Don't forget about attic space or rafters; take advantage of these areas overhead to give your main rooms a clutter-free appearance. You can also add storage space beneath a floorboard. Call in a contractor or handyman to figure out the best place to carve out a nook for storing items that you rarely use.

🌿 **GO SHOPPING.** There is a multitude of options in home furnishings and accessories that will assist you in maintaining a pared-down look. Baskets and decorative boxes—fabric, wood, metal, or wicker—are quick and easy fixes for keeping the mess in check. Or consider pieces that do double duty, such as a chest or trunk that can hide knickknacks, games, or blankets while serving as a coffee table.

In the end, when your home has a Zen-like atmosphere, you surely won't remember the odds and ends you eliminated in order to achieve the restful mood.

If you find that you do have a lot of items that you simply can't live without, make sure you have plenty of storage space. In the kitchen, take advantage of every space possible. Build cabinets that go all the way to the ceiling; include a pantry for storing dry goods and cleaning supplies; install drawers that pull out rather than cabinets so that you'll be able to reach everything. In the bathroom, if space is at a premium, consider such features as an over-the-toilet fixture that includes shelves or a cabinet. Wicker baskets or fabric boxes, available at retail stores, will help to organize knickknacks. Similarly, in your main living spaces, keep as much stored away as possible to achieve a clean look.

### stepping out

The connection with nature plays a large role in creating a tranquil retreat. Ideally, your cottage will provide easy access to the outdoors. What could be lovelier than passing from your living room through a set of elegant French doors to a patio adorned with simple furnishings? Perhaps you prefer a more modern design, with sliding glass doors leading from your bedroom to a private deck.

Either way, once outside, there should be plenty of places to enjoy outdoor living. If you're building a new cottage, be sure to ask your architect to position decks or patios to make the most of the view. Adorn your outdoor rooms with such comforts as hammocks, swings, and other furnishings that let you relax. Whether you like to bask in the sunlight on a chaise longue or read quietly in a hammock, you should outfit your outdoor space with the same care and attention that you give your indoor rooms.

*left:* Overlooking the water, a deck offers plenty of seating for admiring the view. The black rocking chairs allow the vivid colors of the flowering plants to pop. And the coordinating black side tables make entertaining easier—guests can enjoy a light snack or a drink while they relax and chat.

*right:* Located in an out-of-the-way spot, a hammock invites peaceful daydreaming. To maximize use of this delightful amenity, situate it on a covered porch rather than in the yard—that way you can still enjoy its soothing embrace during rainy weather. A couple of potted plants placed in the corner add color to this minimalist outdoor room.

There are, of course, practical concerns to take into account as you furnish your outdoor area. If you have a deck or patio, you may want to incorporate an awning to provide relief from the sun. This protective device has the added bonus of injecting a decorative flair into the setting. To avoid having to bring seat cushions inside during inclement weather, employ ones that are water-resistant. Or forgo cushions altogether and use furnishings with weather-resistant webbing. Many cottage dwellers select outdoor fabrics that complement the palette of the interior. Taupes, beiges, and whites will certainly set a restful tone, but you may be better off with a darker color to camouflage any dirt or spills. Outdoor pieces are currently available in a wide variety of materials—wicker, teak, cedar, cast iron, and aluminum—and styles. So whether you want a Zen-like low wooden table or a traditional white wicker set, you'll be able to find outdoor furnishings that suit your taste.

To achieve the utmost in tranquillity, design your deck or porch to provide you with a multisensory experience. While you obviously want to arrange your furnishings to take in the best possible view, think about how various sounds and scents can enhance your time outdoors. Along these lines, incorporate fragrant potted plants to allow their sweet aromas to waft over you and perhaps a small fountain to soothe you with the lullaby of trickling water. The result: a refreshing place that allows you to get away from it all, even if only temporarily.

# DINING ALFRESCO

*opposite:* Who wouldn't spend most of their time outdoors with this comfortable setup? A small table surrounded by four chairs provides the ultimate spot for alfresco dining or just relaxing after a day at the beach. The umbrella shades those who want to stay away from the sun's rays.

There's nothing like fresh air to enhance your dining experience. For some, outdoor dining is a favorite part of cottage life. To create a delightful setting where you can feel the warmth of the sun and absorb your natural surroundings while enjoying a leisurely meal, you need only follow a few simple steps.

First, find the perfect location. The optimal spot is situated just off the kitchen, making it easy for the cook to bring the food outside and clean up once everyone is finished. If you're designing a new cottage, include French or sliding glass doors to give access to the outdoors as well as to provide lovely views for the chef.

For a casual atmosphere, a deck or patio will offer a fine locale for enjoying a barbecue or even an ad hoc lunch. Outdoor "kitchens" have become a huge trend, as they facilitate entertaining. Grills now offer gas burners, rotisseries, and smoker trays. Plus, many homeowners are including outdoor refrigeration in their designs.

Whether you plan to serve a gourmet meal or just a snack, you'll want the setting to foster a sense of tranquillity. On a deck, consider incorporating built-in benches along the sides of your space in addition to a table and chairs. The benches will provide extra seating as well as a streamlined look. For a patio, rather than creating a rectangular space,

design one in an organic form to better meld with the natural surroundings. Set some potted flowering plants adjacent to the entry and along the perimeter to give your outdoor dining spot a touch of color. These plants can also be moved indoors when you're entertaining inside.

Don't forget to take comfort into consideration as you design your deck or patio. Consider a table that has an umbrella to shield diners from the strong rays of the sun. Because sunlight can eventually take its toll on umbrellas, as well as seat cushions, you may want to select ones that feature fade-resistant fabrics.

For a more formal setting, outfit a front porch with a small table and chairs to create an intimate spot for tea or an evening snack. A covered porch will allow you to enjoy dining outdoors even if there's a light drizzle. And if your dining spot is sheltered from inclement weather, you can feel secure in bringing out delicate accessories, such as fine linens, silverware, and glassware. (Always avoid using glassware in places where people may be barefoot, such as around a pool.)

As you strive to create a sense of serenity in your outdoor dining area, follow the same guidelines as those mentioned for the indoors: incorporate low-maintenance furnishings and keep it simple.

# chapter two

# Romantic

$\mathscr{S}$PACES SPILLING OVER WITH FLORAL FABRICS AND SIMPLE BUT ELEGANT FURNISHINGS, EXTERIORS BOASTING INTRICATE ARCHI-

TECTURAL DETAILS, AND AN ABUNDANCE OF PLANTS CREATING A LUSH FEELING BOTH INSIDE AND OUT—THESE ARE THE INGREDIENTS

FOR A ROMANTIC COTTAGE. BY SETTING THE STAGE WITH THESE ENCHANTING FEATURES, YOU CAN CREATE A DREAMY HAVEN THAT

DELIGHTS THE SENSES AND WARMS THE HEART. A GETAWAY THAT EXUDES CHARM IS SURE TO PLEASE ALL ITS INHABITANTS.

## home sweet home

*page 36:* How to achieve a romantic ambience? Floral pillows, a weathered table, muted pastels, and a cushioned window seat are the answers for this cottage. *page 37:* Located in Provence, this retreat offers classic French country appeal. Climbing roses bathe the diminutive abode in romance, while burnt sienna walls and periwinkle shutters extend a cheerful greeting. *opposite:* Positioned just beyond a picket fence, a bucolic English cottage features a sloping thatched roof and painted terra-cotta walls. A garden of brightly colored flowers contributes greatly to the picturesque scene.

If you are searching for a romantic retreat, you will want the architecture to reinforce the mood. Similarly, if you're building a new cottage, there are certain features that you should consider including. First, think about the overall structure of the house. What do you want the front entrance to look like? What architectural elements imbue a cottage with charm and storybook appeal? Look to American Queen Anne–style cottages for inspiration. Stemming from the Victorian period, these dwellings boast highly ornamented entryways, posts, and turrets. The latter especially give an exterior a fairy-tale quality—think of Rapunzel letting down her hair from the turret's window. Although she lived in a castle rather than a cottage, the sense of romance is still the same.

Wraparound porches also offer a romantic effect. Picture a porch outfitted with an inviting swing, a grouping of white-painted wrought-iron chairs around a table set for afternoon tea, and a host of flowerpots overflowing with geraniums. The way these porches envelop the whole house offers a sense of warmth.

For some, images of European country cottages spring to mind when thinking about romantic retreats. Whether the location is England or the south of France, these havens evoke warmth through their use of natural colors and materials. Picture an intimate house with a stone facade, set beneath the trees and approached by way of a winding dirt path lined by beds of flowers. Or imagine a brick abode with a quaint thatched roof overhanging the structure to offer shelter. The colors of the natural materials further enhance the romantic mood. The warm reds of brick complement the natural tones of the earth. And the colors visible in stone, which can offer blue and green casts, change as the sun rises and sets.

In addition to the construction and materials, pay close attention to details. Incorporating French doors offers

*opposite:* Diamond-paned windows give romantic airs to a stone cottage softened by blue trim. The dwelling enjoys a lush backdrop provided by a canopy of trees. *right:* Scrolling details, intricate cutouts, and Gothic-style doors are all features typical of a gingerbread-style house. Also typical of Victorian cottages are pastel colors and hanging baskets filled with festive blooms. Here, the rocking chairs not only add visual interest but also offer a great place to enjoy a cool glass of lemonade on a warm day.

elegance and charm, while adding stained glass produces spellbinding effects as sunlight streams through the cottage. Diamond panes of glass, like those from the Victorian era, provide an air of distinction.

Other details that have a big impact include the moldings, trim, and paint colors. Cottages with intricate gingerbread trim along the eaves project a powerful sense of romance. These scrolling elements, combined with a steeply pitched roof that beautifully punctuates the horizon, seem to have leaped from the pages of a fairy tale. As for color, consider feminine pastel hues for the trim. These light tints will have a fanciful and eye-catching effect.

## colors, patterns, materials

The exterior architecture of the cottage sets the stage for what is to come, hinting at the mood of the rooms that lie inside. If the structure has good bones—well-placed windows, plenty of nooks and alcoves, and an abundance of architectural details such as crown moldings and chair rails—it's easy to give your rooms an air of romance.

The colors, patterns, and materials in your living spaces will go a long way toward setting the desired mood. Certain patterns, such as those with garden airs, are particularly evocative of a romantic aesthetic. For an upbeat look, incorporate fabrics and wall coverings with floral or vinelike designs. When you enter a living room that's outfitted to look like you've just stepped into a garden, you're sure to enjoy the setting. Imagine gathering with a couple of friends for an afternoon of quiet conversation in a room decked out with a plush sofa and wing chairs covered with the likes of pink peonies or red roses and green leaves. If you prefer a more subtle approach, upholster furnishings in delightful toiles; their bucolic scenes will infuse the space with simple charm, while their restraint in color will provide an air of elegance.

For your dining room, consider selecting wallpaper that has swirling vines so that you feel like you're surrounded by nature as you linger over delicious meals. Chairs covered in rose-colored chintz will introduce a touch of refinement while maintaining the romantic mood. A more casual fabric, such as green-and-white striped ticking, also fits in with the surroundings while adding a refreshing quality to the room. Situations both formal and informal call for a floral centerpiece to adorn the table.

The bright hues in these gardenscapes enliven spaces and energize visitors. Color experts theorize that people respond

*opposite:* Dining in this setting is like a breath of fresh air. Dainty-looking wrought-iron furnishings, traditionally found on a patio, imbue the room with alfresco airs, while a verdant centerpiece and a colorful floral table runner heighten the effect. Overhead, a chandelier provides a final romantic flourish.

*left:* It's easy to add romantic touches. Try arranging a tray with such items as antique-looking silver pieces, candles, and flowers. Consider placing a floral napkin, fabric, or even decorative paper on the surface of the tray to give it a bit of color.

to reds with excitement because the hue has such a vibrant quality. For a romantic scheme, lively colors work well, but pastels, those Easter egg–like shades, are also appropriate. Be careful not to get carried away with pattern, though, as excessive use will overwhelm the space. If you've selected a floral couch and chairs for a room with patterned wallpaper, you may want to keep your window treatments and rugs simple. Solid-colored sheers or off-white lace curtains will contribute a light and airy note to the space. For floors, try a solid-colored carpet or a muted needlepoint rug that complements the other hues in the room. If your furnishings are

the main event in terms of color and pattern, you may want to forgo busy wallpaper and paint your walls instead. White walls are not boring if there is enough going on in the rest of the space. Remember that a jumble of too many patterns and colors can appear dizzying rather than pleasing.

Colors are always affected by lighting. In the morning, when the sun streams through your windows, you may not need a lot of artificial light. In general, soft lighting will best enhance a romantic setting, though work areas require direct task lighting. Victorian sconces with glass shades will present a sentimental touch of yesteryear in a living room.

# MIXING PATTERNS

*If you love the look of rooms filled with patterns but are afraid to try this in your own cottage, take heart. Below are some tips to help simplify the process.*

*opposite:* This living room brings together an array of patterns with beautiful results. What's the secret? For starters, the patterns all include the same coloration. They are also used as accents against a neutral backdrop.

**THINK ABOUT ALL THE ELEMENTS IN THE ROOM.** Before you purchase even a throw pillow, consider your scheme as a whole. Decide in advance what patterns you'll be using for walls, rugs, furnishings, draperies, and accessories.

**LIMIT THE NUMBER OF PATTERNS.** The best rule of thumb is to use from three to five patterns in one room. The smaller the room, the fewer patterns you should use.

**CONSIDER SCALE.** If you're using a large floral print on your sofa, for example, find a more subtle pattern like a small check for a side chair or for pillows. Get swatches of the different fabrics and the wallpaper you're planning to use, and cut them in relation to how they'll be employed. For example, make your wallpaper the biggest swatch, since this will be covering the largest area. Then you can get a more accurate sense of how these patterns will work together.

**PICK A FOCAL POINT.** Decide which element in your scheme should have the most importance. If it's your sofa, that is the piece that should bear the dominant print.

**THINK ABOUT TEXTURE.** The weights of the fabrics will affect the way the patterns mesh. Again, it's important to put all your samples together before making a final decision.

**TRY A MONOCHROMATIC SCHEME.** If you stick to one color along with white or a neutral, you'll be less likely to make a mistake. Take blue and white, for instance; using these time-honored colors, you could adorn a guest bedroom with striped wallpaper, a diamond-patterned rug, and perhaps toile bedding.

**TAKE THE SIZE OF THE SPACE INTO CONSIDERATION.** You're better off with paler tones in small rooms, but you can be quite bold and use more patterns in large spaces.

**TRICK THE EYE WITH PATTERN.** If you're considering a checked floor in your kitchen, set the checks diagonally to make the space seem bigger. In your living room, try a trompe l'oeil print on the walls to give the area a sense of depth.

**ASK FOR HELP.** Hiring a designer, of course, will pay off. However, if this is not in your budget, many companies offer lines of coordinating patterns, which include wall coverings, upholstery, and drapery fabrics.

**TRUST YOURSELF.** Your judgment about what will work is probably right. And remember: you are the one who will have to live in these spaces.

And a romantic dining room practically cries out for a chandelier, perhaps with paper shades or tassels. When it comes time to set the table for an intimate dinner, don't forget the candles. In fact, candles can be sprinkled throughout the cottage to infuse the interior with a romantic ambience (just be sure not to leave them unattended). On a similar note, placing kerosene-style lamps around rooms will bring a warm glow to interiors. By designing spaces where all the elements complement one another, you'll fill your interior with a beautiful sense of harmony.

## pretty pieces

Once you have your color scheme and an idea of what materials you like, you can begin selecting the furnishings. Start with the living spaces—the places where you'll be entertaining, enjoying family gatherings, or just relaxing. First and foremost, you'll want these rooms to be comfortable. Plenty of plush furnishings and an efficient layout are key. For your living room, decide if you would like a casual or more formal setting—either can be made to look romantic. If you prefer a laid-back atmosphere, consider loose-fitting slipcovers and accessories that bear a pleasingly timeworn appearance. If something more refined is to your liking, a tailored look can be achieved with upholstered pieces featuring buttons, fringe, or tassels. Either way, choose pieces that are downright pretty and offer a feminine quality. If you have the space, consider purchasing a fainting couch. A long, sleek piece like this is sure to add drama to any space. But perhaps you prefer a cozy armchair accompanied by a tufted ottoman—an arrangement that welcomes guests to sit down for a spot of tea. Keep in mind that an ottoman needn't be used solely as a footrest; you can also put one into service

as a coffee table. To make this upholstered piece more practical, place a tray on top, allowing you to safely rest a drink on it. In general, make sure you have plenty of side tables for setting down a book or a snack, stationing a lamp, and displaying cherished photos and small floral bouquets.

To make your living room feel more intimate, group your furniture accordingly, creating multiple conversation areas.

*opposite:* This sitting area is budding with romance, thanks to the many floral motifs. Slipcovered chairs suggest an easygoing mentality. *above:* Flea-market finds, such as an antique mirror and a delightful piece used as a fireplace screen, give this room character.

# AFTERNOON TEA

A tea party—whether impromptu or planned—is a lovely way to spend an afternoon. If you decide to host such a gathering, the first step is to determine the venue. Will the weather hold up, allowing you to set up a table and chairs on your lawn? Or would you rather play it safe by staying indoors? If the weather is just a little damp, a covered porch will permit you and your guests to enjoy the fresh air while being shielded from the drizzle.

If you're on the lawn, find a level area on which to station your table and chairs; you don't want your table or seating to wobble around while visitors are drinking hot tea. Try to ground your furnishings so that they are stable. If you're inside, make sure that you have enough room to serve your guests effortlessly.

Whether you have a wrought-iron table and chairs or a set made of wicker, you'll want to adorn the pieces with just the right touches. Place cushions on chairs to make them more comfortable; cover your table with the perfect linens, perhaps ones with a strawberry or ladybug pattern to offer a hint of whimsy; and top the whole arrangement off with a riveting centerpiece. The centerpiece may be as simple as a clear glass vase filled with tulips just picked from your garden or a more intricate creation, such as a rose topiary with a French wire ribbon bow tied at its base. As an alternative to a single centerpiece, you might elect to situate individual bud vases containing a few small blooms at each place setting—these can double as favors for your guests to take home. Once you've set the scene, it's time to make some freshly brewed tea and perhaps some bite-size cucumber sandwiches.

*above:* This Victorian-style gazebo offers a charming setting for a small tea party. A cozy settee joins two white wicker chairs for an element of surprise, while a small table dons a lacy white cloth in honor of the occasion. Keep in mind that a tea party does not have to include hot beverages and finger sandwiches; iced tea and fruit can provide a refreshing alternative during warm weather. *opposite:* For a more formal afternoon tea, dress up the scene with gleaming silver, elegant china, and luxuriant roses. This sunny alcove provides the best of both worlds, granting visitors the feeling of being outdoors yet protecting them from the elements.

Set up your main area with a sofa, a table (or an ottoman), and side chairs in the center of the space. If there is a hearth, take advantage of it and arrange your furnishings so that you and your guests can enjoy the warmth of the fire and gaze upon the mesmerizing flames. Once you've got your main conversation area established, create a smaller gathering spot with another table and some seating—perhaps a card table, located beneath a window, with two small chairs. If there isn't that much square footage, consider incorporating a bench with a cushion or a window seat. These extra conversation areas will provide hours of enjoyment.

The same concepts hold true for your eating areas. For the dining room, creating an intimate setting is essential to establishing a romantic mood. Some dining rooms include two small tables rather than one so that guests can be in closer contact. For a European flair, bring in a French-style dining set with ornate carvings or a more rustic trestle table, then fill the room with complementary pieces to enhance the romantic tone. Add a sideboard, one that has a beautifully carved apron and wrought-iron pulls, or find a corner cupboard made of pine. Adorn these storage pieces with collectibles that will contribute to the romantic air—perhaps a host of china teapots passed down from your grandparents. Scour flea markets for Victorian-style dishes and antique brass or pewter candlesticks to complete the room.

Your kitchen will benefit from flea-market finds as well. Time-honored copper pots hung from a rack can bring a French country flavor to the setting, while antique jars and containers lined up on your counters will infuse the area with old-fashioned charm. Additional details such as floral café curtains and wallpaper borders and country apron-style sinks will all promote a romantic ambience.

The private areas of the cottage—the bedrooms and baths—often play second fiddle to the living spaces when it comes to decorating. However, these are the areas that you can really transform into dreamlike settings. After all, what is more romantic than a canopy bed? Draped with fabric or netting, this bed reminds us of childhood fairy tales in which the princess rests peacefully beneath a sheltering canopy. But this is not the only means for injecting a bedroom with romance. Indulge in your decorating fantasies.

*opposite:* This dining room welcomes occupants with slip-covered chairs and a cushioned wicker sofa. Delicate sheers with a floral motif soften the windows to complete the romantic scene. *above:* Don't forget to give your kitchen some decorative attention. Here, a distressed paint treatment—accented by hanging dried flowers—introduces a lovely timeworn look.

*left:* With its sunny palette, this bedroom makes it easy to rise and shine in the morning. The white canopy, bed linens, and curtains show up well against the yellow wall. A rag-rolling technique creates the uneven look of the paint.

*opposite:* A salvaged piece of distressed wood acts as a novel headboard while infusing the space with a romantic sense of history. Old-fashioned bedding with embroidered details heightens the effect, as does a painted night table featuring a floral design. If you don't want to use antique linens, you can achieve a vintage look by tea-staining sheets and pillowcases.

*left:* Think about all the surfaces in your bath. Here, wainscoting, floral wallpaper, and a checkered pattern of tiles combine beautifully. Stained glass windows allow light to stream in, while providing privacy.

*right:* An arch-shaped mirror and a hook for hand towels provide stylish solutions for practical necessities. Other elegant touches include the Victorian-style faucet and the many silver accessories. Navy walls and white paneling establish a refined backdrop while a bouquet of daffodils adds a splash of color.

*opposite:* A claw-foot tub, an elegant chair, and a pair of period sconces infuse this bath with an undeniable sense of femininity. Toile upholstery and floral wallpaper enhance the effect. Notice how the muted tones of the wallpaper pick up the hues of the tub and the chair.

*above:* Latticework enlivens the back wall and the ceiling of this enclosed porch, while a chandelier entwined in floral vines makes a fitting decorative accent. *opposite:* A mix of floral fabrics and wicker furnishings lends this stone patio a casual air. Weathered wooden tables provide resting spots for reading materials and snacks. In the background, painted tulips sprout up from a garden gate.

with a tufted chair for primping in style; skirt side tables with fabric to soften their hard edges; place a freestanding, full-length mirror on the diagonal in a corner; station a cushioned rocking chair by the window; and deck the bed with lace coverlets and ruffled pillows.

For the bath, stick to traditional pieces, such as a pedestal sink or a claw-foot tub, to continue the romantic aesthetic. Then decorate this private retreat with such items as scented soaps, embroidered hand towels, candles, a silver hand mirror, or a collection of perfume bottles.

## outdoor oases

Once you have decorated the interior of your cottage, direct your attention toward the exterior. A porch, especially a wraparound one, provides the ideal framework for a romantic outdoor room. Both wrought-iron and wicker furnishings are appropriate for setting the mood. If you have a wraparound porch, take advantage of the space to create multiple activity areas. For example, position a rocking chair in one corner for reading, a small table and chairs for an alfresco snack at the other end, and a cozy love seat in between for stargazing with a special someone. Don't forget to soften the architecture's edges with plenty of potted plants—hanging overhead, lined up on the floor, or situated on a stand. Bright red geraniums or a pot of white daisies may be just the right touch for your porch.

If you don't have an outdoor room per se, don't be discouraged. Set up a folding table and chairs on your lawn, cover the table with a floral cloth, and top it off with a small vase of flowers or a pillar candle protected by a hurricane shade for an impromptu romantic dinner.

If you've decorated other parts of your cottage to be reminiscent of a garden, you can continue the theme by transforming an old garden gate into a noteworthy headboard. Traditional brass or four-poster beds are sure to add charm as well. Another option is a white-painted iron bed, which offers a clean backdrop for patterned bedding. If you have the room, consider a sleigh bed. While this piece takes up quite a bit of space, it can make a stunning focal point.

Once you've decided upon the bed, add furnishings and accessories that speak of femininity. Set up a dressing table

*opposite:* Amid lush greenery and potted plants, you can carve out a quiet spot to enjoy the great outdoors. White wicker offers a crisp look. And if you like the appearance of wicker, but don't want to be bothered bringing it in and out of the house as weather conditions vary, take heart—today's options include wicker look-alikes that are made of a water-resistant synthetic.

*right:* A European flavor pervades this setting, where the chairs and tablecloth echo the hue of the cottage's shutters for a truly coordinated look. The large table can comfortably accommodate a crowd when the mood to entertain strikes.

# chapter three

## Cozy

*A* COZY COTTAGE PROVIDES A WARM SANCTUARY WHERE YOU FEEL SAFELY HIDDEN AWAY FROM THE WORLD AND

ENSCONCED IN ALL THE COMFORTS YOU COULD EVER WANT OR NEED. THIS INVITING REFUGE WELCOMES VISITORS AT EVERY

TURN—FROM, SAY, AN ENTRYWAY FILLED WITH FAMILY PHOTOS TO A LIVING ROOM BRIMMING WITH COLLECTIBLES AND SINK-

INTO SEATING TO BEDROOMS OUTFITTED WITH PLUSH DOWN COMFORTERS AND LOADS OF PILLOWS. BY DEFINITION COTTAGES

ARE SMALL, BUT RETREATS THAT PROJECT A COZY MOOD OFFER A SENSE OF INTIMACY LIKE NO OTHER.

*page 62:* Cottages by their very nature are small, so why not play up the intimate character of these dwellings? Here, a daybed tucked beneath the eaves creates a snug, secure feeling. Performing as a sofa by day and a bed at night, the versatile piece expands the functions of the room in a space-efficient manner. *page 63:* Mounds of pillows result in a warm and cozy atmosphere. A headboard reminiscent of a picket fence adds country appeal and proves that there's plenty of room for creativity in a small space. *opposite:* With its protective overhanging eaves, this cottage seems to nurture its inhabitants. A dormer window and flower-filled window boxes enhance the home's storybook quality.

## a warm welcome

Modest in scale, a cozy cottage greets visitors and residents with a heartening sense of warmth. While most cottages are small in stature, certain architectural features, such as over-hanging eaves and dormer windows, heighten the intimate quality. Inside, rooms tend to be snug, featuring quirky nooks and alcoves, as well as enticing fireplaces.

Converted outbuildings make particularly cozy havens. Thanks to their past lives, these retreats offer a unique charm that is undeniably appealing. A cottage transformed from a boathouse will boast such intriguing features as octagonal windows and wide openings once used to allow boats to enter. Chicken coops or sheds, with wooden exteriors and small windows, can also be updated to create delightful hide-aways, as can old-fashioned carriage houses. These delightful structures can be designed to serve as fully equipped cottages or simply as guest quarters.

All of these converted outbuildings offer a humble scale as well as a patina of age. Together, these elements create the groundwork for an inviting retreat. If the original structure doesn't provide enough space to function as a full-fledged dwelling, you can add on—just make sure to maintain the overall small scale. The original building could become a great room, housing a living area, dining area, and kitchen, while a new second level or an addition into the surrounding yard could hold a bedroom and bath. The details, such as the shingles that have weathered to the perfect shade of gray, will give this type of retreat its allure. And if you're expanding one of these treasures, consider recycling wood, perhaps pieces where the paint has worn thin, to create a one-of-a-kind living room floor or a delightful dresser for your bedroom.

Providing a wonderfully cozy shell, these converted struc-tures offer interior details with an abundance of character.

*opposite:* When transforming an outbuilding into living quarters, pay attention to exterior and interior details. Here, a garden shed takes on new life as a guest bedroom with such inviting features as French doors, painted shutters, and planters over-flowing with colorful blooms. A sign above the entrance pays tribute to the garden location.

*right:* Inside, the tiny cottage is filled with homey touches and garden accents. Shelves display worn flowerpots, flea-market finds, and other special trinkets. Luscious hydrangeas in greens and whites bring nature's bounty indoors.

*opposite:* There's nothing that says a small guest cottage can't have all the comforts of home. Here, a cloudlike bed, a wooden chair outfitted with plump cushions, and a charming fireplace stand ready to pamper guests. A creamy palette not only offers a stylish look, but makes the space seem larger. *right:* To make a room feel more intimate, turn to color. Here, claret red walls add visual warmth to a living room. The same hue is picked up in the throw pillows, table, and lamp. Even the diminutive floral arrangement features red, orange, and yellow for a radiant glow.

A kitchen with unfinished wood walls and wood rafters is sure to be a place where the cook will enjoy fixing meals. And the cozy work space will draw friends and guests to help in the preparation of food or to simply keep the cook company. Bedrooms that are diminutive in scale with proportionately sized windows give their inhabitants a sense of security and warmth. Try to maintain the original structure's personality by keeping the existing elements and just updating them so that the space is livable.

## casual comfort

Warm colors, oversize furnishings, and an abundance of accessories are the key ingredients of a cozy setting. The most successful interiors are those that feature a layering effect. When trying to achieve this in your own cottage, work from the outside in, from big to small. You'll want to think about walls, floors, and window treatments, then tackle furniture, lighting, and accents.

Throughout your spaces, the colors should be rich. You might want to paint your dining room a deep orange and

*opposite:* A sumptuous chocolate hue envelops this bedroom for a cozy feeling. Although small, the space exudes a sense of luxury, thanks to the flowing window treatment, the floral throw draped over the chair, and the pile of velvet-trimmed pillows.

*right:* What better place to curl up with a good book than in a cushy armchair surrounded by "a few" of your favorite things? Every inch of this snug corner is adorned with decorative objects for a homey rather than cluttered look. Practical needs are attended to, as well; a floor lamp offers light for reading, a faux-bamboo table stands ready to hold a cup of tea, and an ottoman invites stretching out and reclining.

employ a golden yellow for the living room. For the bath, why not try a muted red, perhaps auburn, for the walls? In general, hues that have warm undertones—ones with more red in them than blue—help to promote a cozy ambience. A golden yellow will make you feel as if you've walked into a sun-filled space, while a deep orange has the power to evoke thoughts of a glorious autumn day. To give the colors a varied effect, you can use paint techniques, such as rag-rolling or sponging. In a dining or living area, a textured paint treatment in a sunbaked shade of terra-cotta can transport residents and guests to the countryside of Tuscany. If

you're not up to the task of trying a paint technique, wallpapers that mimic these effects are readily available.

Window treatments go a long way toward making your interiors feel warm and snug. For the most powerful impact, you'll want to dress windows with a heavy hand. For example, you could pair red-and-white checked café curtains with a solid or striped valence to add warmth to your kitchen. In the dining room, you could try installing warm-toned wood blinds, softened by golden-hued draperies that have enough fabric to create a billowy effect. To make a room cozy, it's important to consider the materials chosen for your window

*right:* **More than a dozen pillows line this sofa to create a plush look. Rich colors and textures further enhance the living room.**

treatments. Picture a deep eggplant velvet drape in the bedroom or a nubby woven fabric gracing windows in the living room. The more fabric and the more tactile, the better.

Underfoot, you'll probably want plenty of floor coverings to heighten the sense of coziness. If your cottage is by the water, opt for rugs rather than wall-to-wall carpeting, because sand that's dragged in from the beach can easily be shaken out of a rug (thereby freeing you from the need for constant vacuuming). Plus, if your living and dining areas cohabit in an open-plan space, rugs can help visually define the individual zones. Even in your kitchen and bath, make

sure to include throw rugs to warm up the areas. Rather than choosing a tightly woven rug like a sisal, select a floor covering that will reinforce the cozy feeling—rugs and carpets with cut pile provide substantial cushioning for bare feet.

Once you've designed the shell of your interior, it's time to think about your furniture. What will make your rooms feel cozy? Overstuffed furnishings—with their massive presence and luxurious sense of comfort—are a good place to start. When you arrive at your cottage after a long drive, you'll want a couch that you can just melt into or an armchair—paired with an ottoman to prop up weary feet—that's

# DOUBLE-DUTY FURNISHINGS

*Cozy cottages are delightful, but perhaps not always practical. To make the most of their snug interiors, find furnishings that can perform more than one function. Here are a few longtime favorites.*

*above:* This platform bed is designed to provide extra storage. The drawers beneath the mattress are great for bulky sweaters, and the smaller drawers off to the side are perfect for stowing gloves and scarves.

**DAYBEDS.** A living room can easily host overnight guests with the help of a daybed. Set against the wall and lined with toss pillows, this versatile furnishing provides extra seating for family and friends during waking hours. At night, it can be outfitted with bed linens to offer a place to sleep.

**BLANKET CHESTS.** Useful in almost any room, these clever pieces can play a number of roles simultaneously. In the living area, a blanket chest can be used as a coffee table as well as storage space for magazines and books. In a bedroom, set the chest at the foot of the bed and place a cushion on top for additional seating. Fill the chest with your sweaters in the summer and your T-shirts in the winter.

**NESTING TABLES.** If you're short on space, consider replacing your end table with a group of nesting tables. Sold in sets of three, these tables in graduated sizes offer plenty of versatility. For instance, when you're entertaining, they can be drawn out and used as stations for food, plates, and napkins. When the party's over, they can easily be stashed under one another again for space-efficient storage.

*above:* Your eating areas should be just as welcoming as the other rooms in your cottage. The inclusion of such items as slipcovered wing chairs and extra pillows will make dining a regal experience for you and your guests.

reading a book. When it's time to go to bed, you retreat to a master suite that has all the creature comforts your heart could desire: an airy duvet, flannel sheets, plush draperies, and an abundance of soft pillows. As a general rule, try to use materials that feel comforting to the touch—flannels, velvets, chenille, cashmere—throughout your rooms to heighten the sense of warmth.

## *accessories*

Less is *not* more for a cozy retreat. You want to create a very lived-in look. Filling your rooms to overflowing with comfortable furnishings, charming accessories, and collections steeped in sentiment will go a long way toward achieving this effect. You'll want to have plenty of space to display objects you've gathered over the years—ones that bring back fond memories and have stories to tell. These cherished possessions will bring a personal touch to your cottage.

In your living area, incorporate plenty of shelves to show off prized collectibles; drape lace coverings over sideboards; and scatter small tables throughout the room, topping them with lamps, framed photos, bud vases, and other treasures. You could also place a stack of books (the height of a side table) beside a chair and use the flat surface as a resting spot for other special objects.

Take a similar approach in the dining area, and incorporate plenty of display surfaces such as hutches, sideboards, and corner cupboards with open shelving. To encourage diners to linger over meals, outfit chairs with comfortable cushions or tie-on pillows.

In the kitchen, put everything on display by employing open rather than concealed storage. Hanging pot racks, wine cubbies, corner display niches, and plate racks are highly efficient when space is tight and allow items to remain on view.

perfectly sized for relaxing and watching television. And don't forget the accessories. A plethora of throws and mounds of pillows, in both living areas and bedrooms, promise warmth, comfort, and a reassuring sense of security for all.

Consider the textures of the materials you select. A fuzzy cashmere throw—easily accessible atop a sofa back—will be a delight to touch. Picture yourself on a cold night curled up in the overstuffed chair, covered by the soft blanket, and quietly

# SOFT TOUCHES

*above:* Comforting touches pervade this corner with plenty of tactile fabrics. A plush rug adds warmth, while the textural slipcover gives the chair a cozy quality. Finally, sheers at the window lend an open and airy feeling to the room.

Upholstered furnishings and layers of textiles are some of the main ingredients of cozy retreats. But in order to ensure the utmost in comfort, pay special attention to the material and construction of the fabrics you choose. You'll want to make sure that they are of the appropriate weight and that they're soothing to your skin—not scratchy or itchy.

A soft, fuzzy throw may be just what you need to keep warm while you're watching television in your living room; it can also be draped over a side chair in the dining room to warm up the space visually and provide a splash of color. What are your options in materials? A cotton throw is a perfect summertime addition. Since cotton breathes, it is a lighter type of throw. For something a bit warmer, consider cashmere. Made of wool from the cashmere goat, it offers a luxurious hand. Angora, which generally comes from a rabbit, also provides a silky texture. All of these choices may come as a blend. Oftentimes, blends are more durable and cost less.

Also think about what types of fabrics and materials you want on your bed. Today's options are endless. From down comforters to crisp sheets, you'll need to scour the stores before you make your decision. Here, too, the materials will offer different levels of warmth. Sheets made with linen are cool in the summer, but they generally need to be dry-cleaned. Flannel offers a cozy option, but may be too hot for some. In the middle ground, you'll find the most common choice—woven cottons. These can come as jacquards, where a design is woven into the sheet, or prints, where the pattern is, not surprisingly, printed onto the fabric. Cotton knits are also available in a variety of colors.

*opposite:* When space is tight, storage is key. Here, open shelves not only provide a place for books and decorative objects, but also allow these items to add visual interest. A metal trunk serves as both a coffee table and a place to stow less attractive items. *right:* Hanging copper pots, wood counters, and exposed beams imbue this kitchen with warmth, while open shelves put dishes and serving pieces—decorative in their own right—on display. One can almost envision a big family breakfast served on the country-style table.

*right:* A small bath benefits from a series of shelves. The handy unit effortlessly accommodates extra towels, soaps, and toiletries, not to mention a few decorative accents. With everything on view, items are easy to find. A pedestal sink gives an air of elegance while taking up little space.
*opposite:* To add character to a room, include plenty of accessories. In this bedroom, a collection of blue-and-white plates presides over the bed, taking the place of the traditional painting or mirror. A chest used to store out-of-season clothes doubles as a display surface for a number of objects, including an oar.

As in your living areas, covering every surface will further the cozy mood. Toward that end, adorn windowsills with a collection of salt and pepper shakers, vintage green glass bottles, or potted herbs; line counters with tins and canisters for storing dry goods; and use the area above the cabinets to hold baskets or large serving trays—doing so will free up the cabinets below for smaller items.

For baths, add warmth with not only rugs but plush towels as well. Be creative with storage and display features. For example, if you don't have room for a linen closet, roll up towels and place them in a basket, or consider buying an over-the-toilet unit. These are available at many bedding retailers, and they provide an extra place for such sundries as perfume bottles, decorative figurines, and toiletries. Hang a collection of antique mirrors to finish off the look.

Similar ideas work well in the bedroom. Velvet draperies, thick comforters, soft rugs, and bookshelves filled to the brim all work together to create a cozy space. And don't forget your walls; cover these with family photos, artwork, and collections. Use picture ledges, cantilevered shelves, or hanging devices for more unusual ways of displaying your favorite pieces.

# BREAKFAST IN BED

You awake on Sunday morning and instead of having to get ready for work and send the kids off to school, you are free to relax and enjoy your breakfast in the privacy of your bedroom. A simple breakfast tray placed on top of your bed will always do the trick, but why not indulge a little? Include a small table and two chairs in the corner of your room, perhaps under a window. If you don't have enough space to leave a table and chairs out at all times, consider a table that folds up or one that you can wheel from a larger area into your bedroom.

If you're remodeling or building a new house, you might include a built-in dresser that features a refrigerator drawer. Designed to look like an ordinary drawer for sweaters, this amenity doesn't take up much space—it's just extra deep. You can keep your favorite breakfast treats fresh for your private repast in this clever storage space.

No matter how grand or casual your breakfast in bed, you can make it special. Have a tablecloth at the ready; cut a flower from your garden or steal one from another arrangement and place it in a bud vase to give color to your table or tray; place a collection of small jams on a plate; and use your favorite dishes. Your welcoming setup is sure to provide a short respite from the fast pace of everyday life.

*right:* What could be more delightful than rolling out of bed and enjoying a morning meal? Here, a small table helps to make this dream a reality. When the table is not needed for breakfast, it can be moved off to the side and used as a desk.

*right:* Although the space is small, the atmosphere is extremely welcoming. The architecture alone offers great character, but the wash of sunny yellow paint and the abundance of flowers bring a smile to one's face. A rustic chair suits the surroundings and invites visitors to sit for a spell and reflect upon nature. *opposite:* Plush chairs, a plethora of pillows, and layers of textiles bring a cozy, luxurious feeling to this enclosed porch.

## under the sun

Whether it's a hot day or a cool night, you'll want your porch or deck to reflect the comfort of your interiors. Your outdoor rooms can be just as cozy. If you have an open area, bring in a sheltering awning or umbrellas to create a sense of enclosure and security. Then, establish intimate conversation areas. Setting chairs catercorner offers a friendly, casual atmosphere and promotes interaction. Next, wherever possible, make your outdoors more comfortable. Add cushions to a bench or pillows on top of dining chairs. Finally, make sure to have plenty of potted plants to create a lush feel. These can be easily shifted around or removed and replaced when you want a quick change of scenery; plants can also be arranged to shield your outdoor area from the prying eyes of neighbors or passersby, thereby providing some treasured privacy.

*left:* A postage stamp–size terrace becomes an alluring spot for quiet conversation. While the furnishings consist of the bare necessities—two comfortable chairs and a small table—the decorative details give the space its warmth and charm. A golden hue bathes the compact area in a radiant glow, while flowering vines create a sensuous canopy overhead. *opposite:* Wherever possible, include cozy conversation areas. Guests and family will love these spaces—especially if they're outdoors. On this deck, two white wicker chairs with plenty of cushions flank a matching occasional table to create an enticing setting for a tête-à-tête. The red, white, and blue scheme offers a cheerful, crisp look, and a low-maintenance rug adds comfort underfoot.

chapter four

# Nostalgic

*I*F YOU YEARN FOR THE SIMPLER LIFE OF DAYS GONE BY, THEN PERHAPS A NOSTALGIC TONE IS WHAT YOU HOPE

TO ACHIEVE IN YOUR COTTAGE RETREAT. FOR MANY, THIS TRANSLATES TO A REFRESHING COUNTRY-STYLE DECOR. WITH

THEIR UNPRETENTIOUS FORMS AND TRADITIONAL YET CASUAL DEMEANOR, AMERICAN COUNTRY PIECES—ANTIQUE OR

REPRODUCTION—SEEM WELL SUITED TO THE SLOWER PACE OF COTTAGE LIFE.

*page 86:* Filled with an eclectic mix of furnishings, this room reminds us of days gone by. From the eighteenth century–style chair with cabriole legs to the decorative plates artfully mounted on the wall, it's clear that a sense of nostalgia pervades the space. *page 87:* An antique wagon is put to novel use as storage space for decorative items. The red, white, and blue blankets stack neatly within its confines and add a dash of color against the wood. *opposite:* A converted barn sets the stage for this kitchen's old-fashioned country flavor. Keeping the barn doors intact enhances the charm and offers a spacious opening that can be appreciated on warm summer days.

You can also enhance the nostalgic mood with pieces that carry a personal history for you. Remember your grandparents' house with the furnishings and knickknacks that today evoke wonderful memories? Perhaps you have the rocking chair where your grandmother used to sit and crochet or the hand-painted humidor where your grandfather kept his cherished cigars. Placing these beloved items in your cottage will surely give it an old-fashioned flair while filling it with a sentimental quality. And whether you decide to station that old Singer sewing machine in a corner of your living area or rest an antique bed warmer against a wall in your bedroom, touches of yesteryear will imbue your cottage with charm.

## *first impressions*

Craving a house that evokes times past? Look to classic designs as your guide. American country cottages come in a broad range of shapes and sizes, but they share two key features: simplicity of form and a nod to the past.

For many of those seeking refuge in the country, the answer lies in a farmhouse. Picture the crisp country demeanor of a white clapboard farmhouse with red shutters. If your taste is geared toward a more refined structure, consider a farmhouse with a stone front. Such a dwelling not only offers a traditional look, but also suggests a sense of permanence. If you wish, you can visually soften the hard exterior with strategic landscaping. Let a rosebush with pink blossoms cover some of the gray walls, and add window boxes filled with bright flowers to delight onlookers.

A converted barn is another possibility. With its clean lines and traditional styling, the architecture appeals to many in search of a country retreat. And the lofty space lends itself to an open-plan design—perfect for quality "together time" and entertaining. Last but not least, the structure has loads of character. With a red-painted exterior and white trim, a converted barn surrounded by fields will resemble the subject of an early-twentieth-century oil painting.

*left:* The weathered gray exterior of this converted barn contributes to its appeal. Traditional barn doors preserve the structure's integrity while flanking an entrance that is more typical of a home. *opposite:* The beauty of this cottage lies in its use of materials. Salvaged barn boards make up the walls and offer a patina that you can't get from new wood. The slate floor complements the walls as well as the furnishings within the space. To soften the interior, round braided rugs are placed underfoot, marking the different areas of the dwelling.

No matter what the style of architecture, landscaping is important. Rather than pave your entrance path, for instance, leave it as is. Walking up a dirt path will give your home an old-fashioned flavor. Imagine strolling up that very area and hearing the screen door slam as your mother emerges with a tray of lemonade and fresh-baked cookies. Surround your pathway with beds of beautiful blooming annuals and perennials. Try to incorporate a cutting garden so that you can fill your rooms with the simple, natural beauty of fresh flowers.

## setting the stage

Let the shell of your interior reflect the spirit of country living—in other words, keep it simple. A clean backdrop allows character-filled furnishings and treasures steeped in sentiment to be the main attractions of the space.

For the living room, avoid fussy wallpaper and paint walls a solid color to allow furnishings, artwork, and decorative objects to take center stage. A colorful patchwork quilt—perhaps one lovingly labored over by a member of your family—could hold pride of place hanging above the sofa on a white wall that provides a distraction-free backdrop. If you're afraid that white walls are too bland, enliven them by painting architectural trim such as moldings and window frames in a quiet, muted hue—perhaps a sage green or gray-blue. Of course, white walls are not the only way to go. A solid backdrop of golden mustard or pale blue can also flatter furnishings. And walls featuring beadboard paneling are particularly evocative of country style.

When it comes to floors, if you're fortunate enough to have ones that feature charming wood planking, don't cover them up with wall-to-wall carpeting. Let their natural beauty

shine by using only a small area rug or two where you feel some softening is desirable. Oval rag or braided rugs are sure to give a space a dose of country flavor. If you wish to forgo rugs altogether but want to jazz up your floors a bit, try your hand at the time-honored art of stenciling (or hire a professional to do so). A stenciled floral border, perhaps one featuring cheerful yellow and red blooms, is sure to add a little pizzazz to your space—and keep visitors on their toes—while maintaining a traditional feel.

*opposite:* The shell of your interior should work with your furnishings. Here, rich yellow walls and terra-cotta floor tiles allow a green cupboard and gray ladder-back chairs to pop. *above:* Solid backdrops show off furnishings to great advantage. For variety, set off architectural trim with a different color and change the palette from room to room.

*left:* On your stairs, forgo the traditional runner and try a painted one instead. Here, the muted tones and classic pattern provide subtle embellishment. The result is a sophisticated country look with a nod to the past.

*opposite:* An area rug ties together the colors of this room while supplying cushioning underfoot. Thanks to the rug's small size, the country appeal of the wood-plank floors can still be enjoyed.

*opposite:* Sitting by the fire, curling up with a good book, knitting a sweater—these are some of the simple pleasures in life. And a gracious wing chair provides the perfect spot for engaging in these activities. Upholstered in a lively pattern, this chair exudes a welcoming quality.
*left:* Whether it's Thanksgiving, a family member's birthday, or just an ordinary weekday, this dining room infuses mealtime with a feeling of warmth and nostalgia. A large wooden table provides plenty of room for friends and family, while decorative objects and heirlooms inject personality.

## old-fashioned appeal

If you want to give your rooms a nostalgic feel, think of Norman Rockwell paintings, perhaps those that ran on the covers of *The Saturday Evening Post*. What were the rooms like? What furnishings and materials offer old-time appeal?

For furniture, select pieces that project an old-fashioned tone instead of contemporary airs. For example, choose a sofa with rolled arms rather than one that is streamlined.

Scour antiques markets for country-style pieces such as Windsor chairs or a pine coffee table. When it comes to patterns for upholstery and other fabrics, stripes and checks are longtime favorites. An armchair covered in blue and white ticking stripes may be just the lift your living room needs.

Follow similar guidelines in the dining area. A large harvest table recalls a past when family members all came together for meals—a time when they were not being pulled

# AMERICAN COUNTRY AT A GLANCE

Developing from a need for a more casual way of life, the American country style emerged. Think of the Puritan colonists who settled in New England. These were middle-class people who left England to have a fresh start in the New World. By sheer necessity, their furnishings had to be first and foremost functional, and the materials had to come from readily available resources. Therefore, much of the wood furnishings were made from native American trees such as pine, cherry, and oak. Construction was clean, simple, and geared toward practicality.

Today, utilitarian pieces from our forefathers add a sense of nostalgia to a cottage. The Windsor chair—devised by British cottagers as a sturdy and lightweight seating option and widely adapted by American furniture makers—brings an old-fashioned note to a setting with its bowed back and turnings. Once essential to everyday life, butter churns and spinning wheels can serve as decorative reminders of rural life during colonial times. Handmade accessories such as rag rugs and patchwork quilts also offer country charm.

While country decor went in and out of fashion over the years, there seemed to be a resurgence after America's bicentennial in 1976. Continually being reinterpreted, American country style is evolving. Whether you like the cluttered look of vintage watering cans stacked knee-high or the clean design of a Windsor bench, the key elements of American country remain the same: simplicity and comfort—a style that allows for a casual way of life.

*above:* Classic American country furnishings are simple yet loaded with character. Because of this combination of traits, even the most utilitarian pieces display a unique charm. Here, a ladder used to store books lends a refreshingly quirky sense of style. The cupboard, a more traditional storage provider, offers a sense of nostalgia with its timeworn paint. *opposite:* Attention to detail is what makes certain rooms special. In this bright and cheery eat-in kitchen, painted ladder-back chairs, a wrought-iron chandelier, and an old-fashioned stove are the ingredients for country style.

*right:* With the addition of just a few pieces, a new kitchen boasting all the latest amenities conveys old-fashioned charm. A Hitchcock bench and period light fixtures help bring the past into the present. A freestanding cupboard cuts down on the need for built-in cabinetry and promotes an unfitted look.

in different directions, with kids having late-day soccer practice or orchestra rehearsal and parents working into the evening hours at the office or at home. A massive table such as this encourages folks to gather round, indulge in hearty food, and swap stories about their day. Pewter candlesticks and ladder-back chairs complete the country feeling. For a decorative flair, consider painting the backs of these chairs in different, but harmonious, colors. Alternating between yellow and blue chairs—perhaps with a couple of red ones thrown in—will create an upbeat ring of color around your dining table.

If you have a table that doesn't offer much flair on its own, consider cloaking it in a red-and-white checked tablecloth for a touch of kitsch. If you go this route, unpainted wood chairs, or perhaps Windsor chairs with pine seats and white-painted backs and legs, can make fitting companions. On the walls, consider hanging a collection of blue-and-white china plates instead of traditional artwork.

Lighting—a great mood setter—deserves special attention in the dining room. Candlestick-style sconces will look as though they've been in your home for decades. A wrought-iron chandelier is another fitting touch that will help create the feel of yesteryear.

Fill your kitchen with a sense of nostalgia by incorporating pieces that have an unfitted look. This approach has been an ongoing trend in kitchen design. Cabinet manufacturers are offering more choices so that homeowners can obtain a custom look. And the cabinets seem more like pieces of furniture than stock units. Select features such as plate racks and decorative moldings to create traditional style. Choose a cupboard with an antiqued or distressed finish to hold your favorite heirlooms. Whether you have a collection of all-white

pitchers, vintage bread boxes, or colorful cookie jars, make sure to place these special details on display. The same is true of artwork; find a lively depiction of a rooster or that of a bucolic setting to evoke a country-time flavor.

For the bedroom, select pieces that serve as pleasing reminders of days gone by. A four-poster or brass bed is a good place to start. Whichever style you choose, try topping it off with a jewel-toned antique quilt. The deep purples, warm greens, and muted golds will provide a rich, timeless flair. Set an antique blanket chest at the end of the bed, and call upon a hand-painted wooden dresser to store your clothes. Finish the latter piece off by stationing a pitcher and washbasin on top; creamy white porcelain is optimal if you already have a lot going on in the room, but if you want a

# HIDDEN TREASURES

Have you been saving certain pieces that you found in your grandmother's attic? Are you curious to know if they're worth anything? There are a few ways that you can find out.

Start by examining the piece. See if there are any symbols or markings. In some cases, the manufacturer's name is noted on the piece. If you have something from a well-known manufacturer, such as a Wedgwood bowl, you'll probably be able to obtain information about it rather easily. If you're inspecting a piece of furniture, look at its construction. There are certain features that will help you to determine the age of a piece. For example, if a dresser includes dovetail joints connecting the sides to the top, it's a sign that the dresser is an older piece of casework. (Today those areas are generally connected by dowel construction; dovetails, however, are still used to join the sides of drawers.)

Next, do your research. Take a trip to the library or your local bookstore and look at resources that pertain to your piece. You'll find books on everything from art glass to American furniture. If your piece has some kind of distinctive marking, you'll be able to look that up as well. Antiques experts, including Ralph and Terry Kovel, have written numerous books on how to distinguish markings. Visit Internet sites, too. You can look up online articles regarding your particular subject, as well as visit auction sites, although the latter will not necessarily give you an accurate idea of what your piece is worth. If you're serious about selling your piece, your best bet is to take it to a local dealer. He or she will then examine the item and give you a professional opinion.

Whatever you find out, you may not want to part with a cherished object. Most likely, that old rocking chair you loved as a kid and the box that once held your grandmother's wedding ring are pieces you'll want to keep. After all, you can't put a price on sentiment.

*far left:* Sometimes a room is designed around a family heirloom, like this gracious armoire. An iron bed serves as an airy counterpoint to the massive piece, while proving a worthy companion in terms of scale and elegance. *left:* Show off your treasures to their best advantage. In this quaint bedroom, a collection of china dishes holds pride of place over the bed. Notice how the artful arrangement echoes the contours of the headboard.

Don't overlook your outdoor spaces. These, too, can hark back to yesteryear. The front porch, after all, is a time-honored setting for communing with nature, sharing stories with friends and family, and simply relaxing while savoring the fresh air. Picture a front porch that runs the entire length of the house; its balustrade is painted white, its floorboards a peaceful shade of blue-gray; lined up in a pretty row to take in the view are a few rocking chairs—although the chairs don't match, they are united by a coat of red paint. Off to the side, a quaint porch swing promises hours of enjoyment on warm days and cool summer nights.

Of course, everyone has a unique vision of the ideal outdoor room. If rocking chairs aren't part of your fantasy—or if you don't have a lot of space—you might incorporate hand-painted benches for seating. Pushed up against the side of the house, these pieces allow for a space-efficient layout. When topped with seat cushions, they provide comfortable perches from which family and friends can enjoy one another's company and wave hello to passing neighbors.

When it comes to welcoming decorative touches, the possibilities abound. Consider painting your front door a lively color, such as red. This is sure to extend a warm greeting. Line vintage items, such as watering cans and antique planters, along your porch's boundaries as a final touch.

In your yard, set up a picnic table for quick lunches or evening get-togethers. For a more intimate meal, simply lay a blanket on the grass and bring a picnic basket filled with goodies. Once you're done dining, make sure you have a place you can relax. A simple hammock will certainly enhance time spent outdoors, providing you with a place to close your eyes and think about those special moments of your past, as well as dream about your future.

*above:* Candlestick-style sconces, a decorative rooster, an antique high chair, and painted cabinets infuse this bath with a feeling of yesteryear. *opposite:* Give a fresh look to nostalgic pieces. Here, a porch swing is painted hot pink, making a powerful statement amid the mostly white furnishings. A traditional quilt softens the bold swing and raises the comfort level.

subtle splash of color, find a set that has a blue-and-white or soft red-and-white pattern.

In the bath, let your fixtures help to recall the past. A claw-foot tub not only affords classic appeal but also lends an air of elegance to the room—as does a pedestal sink. Adorn mirrors with antique frames. (Antique mirrors are often no longer usable.) And seek out the perfect light fixtures—perhaps sconces flanking a mirror above the sink—to add that final touch of nostalgia.

# SIMPLE PLEASURES

*Once your cottage has been outfitted with just the right touches, it's time to enjoy the haven you've created. That means taking advantage of the simple pleasures in life.*

**MAKE A SPECIAL MEAL.** Prepare a dish that brings back sweet memories for you and your family. Perhaps it's your grandmother's recipe for pot roast and potatoes or that delicious apple pie that you could smell as you approached her house.

**TAKE THE TIME TO READ A BOOK.** What could be more indulgent than sitting on your porch swing with a glass of lemonade and delving into a novel? Books can take you to far-off lands and allow you to escape your everyday routine, if only for an hour or two.

**HAVE A PICNIC.** Whether you bring wine and cheese or peanut butter and jelly sandwiches, you're sure to enjoy this event with friends or loved ones.

**CREATE MEMORIES WITH YOUR KIDS.** Start a lemonade stand. This old-fashioned tradition never goes out of style. You might even bake some sugar cookies cut into lively shapes. Have your children paint colorful signs, listing the offerings and prices.

**GARDEN.** Even an amateur can enjoy this activity. Go to your local greenhouse to find out what plants will work best in your garden and how much maintenance they'll require.

*opposite:* This humble setting has a comforting air of familiarity. A simple chair situated on a screened porch overlooking the water offers a quiet place to reflect upon days gone by and dream about future aspirations.

*above:* On this wraparound porch, a barrel situated between two Shaker-style chairs takes the place of a traditional table to support a game of checkers. The setting is simple, yet it allows for hours of happy times.

chapter five

# *Rustic*

*S*ET BENEATH A CANOPY OF TREES OR ALONGSIDE A DEEP BLUE LAKE, A COTTAGE IN A WOODED AREA OFTEN WEARS A

RUSTIC LOOK. WHETHER YOU ENVISION A LUMBERJACK'S LOG CABIN OR A CEDAR-SHINGLED LAKESIDE RETREAT, YOU'LL SOON

REALIZE THAT THESE MAN-MADE STRUCTURES ARE DESIGNED TO BLEND HARMONIOUSLY WITH THE NATURAL LANDSCAPE. THIS IS

THE TYPE OF HAVEN TO WHICH ONE MIGHT RETREAT AFTER A DAY OF HIKING, CYCLING, OR WHITE-WATER RAFTING. OR PERHAPS

IT IS SIMPLY A GETAWAY FOR CITY SLICKERS—A SPOT THAT OFFERS PEACE AND QUIET.

*page 110:* Natural materials provide a rusticity like no other. Stone walls, exposed log ceiling beams, and twig furniture are the mood-setting ingredients of this woodland retreat. Perched at the edge of a bluff, the dwelling offers spectacular views. *page 111:* Take advantage of your surroundings. On this enticing deck, two log chairs offer a place to sit and enjoy nature, while an occasional table presents a spot for a cool drink or a snack. *opposite:* This modern interpretation of a log cabin features steeply peaked gables that punctuate the skyline and allow for plenty of glazing on the second level. The more traditional green-painted trim mimics the leaves surrounding the abode.

## one with nature

The American Heritage Dictionary defines the word rustic as "of, or pertaining to, or typical to country life." Just as this is a broad definition, there are many interpretations of rustic style; that is, there is not a singular architectural style that signifies rusticity. So how should you go about designing a cottage with a rustic flavor? First, take a close look at the site. You'll want your getaway to blend in with the natural surroundings. Whenever feasible, try to employ indigenous materials. If this is not possible, select ones that suit the natural elements on the site. A log dwelling will look right at home in the midst of the woods. Similarly, Adirondack-style homes, which feature exposed wood, are well suited to a forest clearing. Even lakeside cottages that include cedar shingles and green-painted trim look as though they belong among the trees. In the mountains, rustic retreats often have a ski-lodge ambience.

Regardless of the particular style, rustic dwellings tend to be simple in terms of both design and materials. They are also generally constructed to withstand harsh weather conditions. The main goals for these structures are to serve their purpose and pay respect to the landscape.

## interior interest

Although a rustic retreat may not come with all the embellishments of a Victorian cottage, it possesses its own intrinsic beauty. The earthy hue of natural wood floors—imagine a rich, honey-colored pine—or exposed wood beams is sure to add warmth to the interior. A massive stone fireplace not only supplies physical warmth, but also offers architectural interest. Even the construction of a home can offer visual appeal. A double-height living room with rafters, for instance, will draw the eye upward. Exposed beams in a bedroom can help create a cozy, cabinlike setting.

*opposite:* This home looks as though it were made from tree branches. Wood moldings climb the walls and beams, and structural supports feature organic shapes. The result is an interior with an outdoor feeling.

*right:* Wood paneling, window trim, and built-in furnishings lend this space a warm glow. Yellow and blue fabrics—with some splashes of red and green—enliven the neutral backdrop.

If you are building or remodeling a rustic retreat, make sure to take full advantage of the views. There's no reason to feel separated from the natural landscape just because you're inside. Allow the living area to merge with the outdoors by incorporating sliding glass doors leading to a wooden deck. Wouldn't it be lovely to have a window right over your kitchen sink, allowing you to gaze upon the breathtaking scenery while preparing a meal or cleaning up? In the bath, if privacy is not an issue, consider installing a window just above the tub to let bathers enjoy the view as they soak.

## rough-and-tumble rooms

Take off your coat, untie the laces of your boots, and relax. A rustic hideaway should be a place where you can unwind after a day of adventures. To get just the right look and feel, you'll want to pay close attention to each and every detail. Start with the entryway; as a preemptive strike against unwanted dirt, you'll probably want to incorporate some sort of mudroom or storage area—a place where family members and guests can shed dirt-caked shoes and wet gear. This small area will make a big difference in helping you to

taking part in and design storage in the mudroom accordingly. To add a bit of flair, paint the bench a fire engine red, or select hooks designed in whimsical shapes. You can also use paint or shelf paper inside the cubbies to give them a visual lift.

Next, take a look at your living room. Here, too, you'll want to maintain a low-maintenance environment. Toward that end, select durable materials—ones that will survive the test of time. Various heavy fabrics not only offer a sturdy construction that stands up to wear and tear, but also contribute visual weight to the setting—a quality that enables these materials to hold their own in rooms where heavy log walls or wood panels prevail.

There are numerous materials suitable for a rustic retreat. Leather, for instance, is a good choice for a no-nonsense cottage. Although pieces upholstered in leather generally cost more, you will get your money's worth, as this material only improves with age. Think of the brown leather chair that has darkened over the years and is wonderfully worn in just the right spots to add character. Another option is denim. Just like a favorite pair of jeans, a denim sofa offers a sense of comfort. And this sturdy fabric is great if you have kids or pets; if you opt for the traditional dark color, many stains will be hidden. Cotton duck—a heavyweight, closely woven fabric—is perfect for a cottage in the woods. Consider purchasing slipcovers in cotton duck or denim so that you can throw them in the washing machine if they get soiled. These handy devices will extend the life of your upholstery.

To fill your rustic retreat with warmth and coziness, outfit it with comfortable, sink-into couches and armchairs. A wing chair positioned next to a floor lamp can encourage quiet reading, while a pair of leather club chairs stationed in

*above:* Low-maintenance furnishings, including a pair of denim-covered chairs, afford this space a sense of ease and comfort.
*opposite:* Leather lends a richness to any room, and actually looks better as it ages.

maintain a hassle-free environment. Outfit this space with such accoutrements as a simple wooden bench where skiers and hikers can take off their boots without fear of toppling over; a series of cubbies to store bicycle helmets, earmuffs, gloves, and other outdoor items; and hooks for coats and jackets. Basically, think about the types of activities you'll be

family and friends the much-appreciated opportunity to prop up their feet after a day of rigorous outdoor activities. Or you could push large ottomans up against the couch for the ultimate lounging experience. Other pieces appropriate for a rustic cottage include those handmade by local craftspeople, such as twig furniture and old-fashioned rockers. If you have a wood-burning stove or a fireplace, create a conversation area around it so that visitors can soak in its warmth comfortably.

Oftentimes, a rustic cottage will have a great room, an open-plan design that includes the living, dining, and kitchen areas. Therefore, you'll want all your furnishings in these distinct areas to work well together. In the dining space, you could include a Mission-style table and chairs or a simple trestle table. These pieces offer clean lines and a rustic simplicity that makes them easygoing companions for other furnishings. To heighten the rustic ambience, include pieces that are unfinished or have a distressed appearance. Next, consider your lighting; an antler chandelier or perhaps a wrought-iron fixture with simple curves might work well over the dining table. A centerpiece of fresh-picked wildflowers arranged in a pitcher or bucket offers a softening touch. You can also inject your personal stamp with such collectibles as stoneware jugs or country-style ceramics displayed in a wooden hutch.

Indeed, it is the decorative accents that will imbue your living spaces with character. Camp memorabilia, such as old-fashioned canteens and vintage fishing gear, enhance the appeal of a rustic retreat while fitting in with the overall tone of the space. Similarly, a "Gone Fishing" sign hanging over your sofa is a refreshing and humorous alternative to traditional artwork. Colorful Pendleton blankets can also enliven

*above:* The furnishings in this dining room take their cues from the woodland setting. Twig chairs surround a table with a base constructed of logs and twigwork. An unusual overhead fixture offers visual interest as well as illumination.

a corner can serve as a secluded spot for an intimate tête-à-tête. What about incorporating a red-and-black checked flannel-covered couch? The lively pattern will complement the simple interior, and the dark colors will hide dirt. Plus, occupants will welcome the soft texture of the fabric. A sturdy log coffee table placed opposite the sofa will give

# MANTEL MAGIC

As the focal point of any living room, the fireplace demands careful decorative attention. When deciding on what to display in this place of honor, take your cues from the locale of your getaway. Are you overlooking a lake? Do you have a mountain retreat that you mainly visit in the wintertime? What are your pastimes? Your answers can guide you to a creative solution. If, for example, your family spends time fishing, you may wish to mount a set of oars above the hearth—find a timeworn pair for rustic character. If cold-weather activities prevail, purchase old-fashioned snowshoes and prop them up on the mantel. Other fitting items might include a collection of pewter plates, hand-painted boxes, or wooden mallards.

*right:* An eclectic mix of furnishings yields great results in this kitchen. Green and red cabinetry gives the subdued earth tones of the space a visual lift, as does cobalt blue tiling running along the edge of the counter. The highlight of the room—a central island—includes a stone base and a wood counter for a naturalistic look, while rooster-back chairs offer a touch of country appeal. *opposite:* Blend old and new. The shell of this kitchen—which includes wood floors, exposed beams, and a log wall—establishes a rustic look, yet the appliances inject a sleek modernity. As a result, the space provides a "getting back to nature" feel without giving up the conveniences of today.

the interior. Think about patterns evocative of Native American styles. You could select pillows with a black, green, and red Navajo-style pattern, or find a colorful rug that has a similar flavor.

Some owners of rustic cottages and cabins take their decorating scheme into a Wild West direction. If you'd like to achieve this look in your own refuge, you could mount a collection of cowboy hats on the wall above the fireplace, place a timeworn saddle on the railing of a second-story balcony overlooking a soaring living room, or accent blue denim drapes with red bandanna tiebacks. These, of course,

are just a few of the many decorative possibilities that you could implement. Use your imagination, and let those creative juices flow.

In the kitchen, adorn your cabinets with a distressed finish, possibly in green, red, or blue. (Indeed, since the shell of your interior will most likely be wood, you can be bold with the colors and accessories you use throughout the home.) If you prefer a more conservative approach, consider giving cabinets a coat of white paint to provide powerful contrast against the wood tones. Then, find window treatments that evoke a country flavor. Curtains made from

bandannas provide a lively effect. Install items both big and small, from ceiling fans to twig-style cabinet hardware, to continue the outdoorsy atmosphere.

For the bedroom, seek out rustic furnishings, such as a large log bed, a wooden dresser with iron pulls, and a bedside table made from a tree stump. Then, illuminate the space with lantern-style lamps to create the sensation that you're camping in the woods. Keep the elements simple, but add warmth with such soft goods as a heavy comforter and a rag rug. Continue to bring in color through your accessories.

You could set a Pendleton blanket at the end of your bed to brighten the space. You could also bring in a ceramic pitcher filled with tall sunflowers.

In the bath, use rich colors against a wood backdrop. Install a red cast-iron tub as your focus, for example. Add antique-looking fittings, perhaps ones that are handheld, to give the tub an old-time flavor. Hang jewel-toned towels atop a twig-shaped towel rack. Find a Navajo or traditional hook rug to give your floors a lift. And be inventive; use a fisherman's vest, for instance, as a place to store toiletries.

*opposite:* Well-appointed furnishings and accessories establish a refined rusticity. All the pieces in this bedroom—the headboard and footboard, the ceiling beams, even the prints—display a rigid geometry. The draping curtains and colorful bedspread, however, bring a soft, feminine touch to the interior. *right:* Less is more when space is tight. Although this bedroom is furnished sparely, it conveys a powerful sense of warmth thanks to the golden hue of the wood walls, floor, and ceiling. A set of cubbies provides the necessary storage, and rugs offer comfortable cushioning.

*left:* A wood cabinet with old-fashioned hardware has been transformed into a vanity. The sink, set into the cabinet, includes classic fittings with cross handles and ivory insets. A pegboard, mounted to the wall, offers a place to hang towels or a basket for stowing toiletries.

*opposite:* Stone floors and log walls transform this bath into a soothing retreat. A curved vanity mimics the shape of the logs for a harmonious effect. Select accessories—simple sconces, a wood-framed mirror, and a wicker basket filled with purple blooms—provide just the right amount of decoration.

*opposite:* Reveling in the great outdoors is truly a universal delight. Here, a deck cantilevers out over the hillside to provide beautiful views of the water below. A bent-willow chair and potted flowering plants are simple additions that fit right in with the natural surroundings.

*left:* A screened porch can be a year-round source of pleasure. The enclosed space admits cool breezes while keeping outdoor pests at bay. Forest green furnishings echo the natural backdrop, while lantern-style light fixtures extend the porch's use into the evening.

## the great outdoors

Maximize time spent outside with the help of such features as screened porches and sprawling decks. These amenities extend your living space—as well as your enjoyment of the outdoors—offering great spots for alfresco dining and peaceful relaxation.

A screened porch has many benefits to offer. For starters, it allows you to enjoy a cool breeze on a summer night without being hounded by pesky mosquitoes. It also allows you to savor the fresh air during a drizzle without getting wet. Picture yourself on a cool spring evening curled up in an Adirondack chair, covered in a warm blanket, as you listen to the soothing sound of raindrops hitting the ground and breathe in the sweet aromas of wet leaves and earth. When outfitted with plenty of comfortable furnishings and softening touches, a screened porch can be a delightful setting in which to while away the hours—playing board games, flipping through magazines, enjoying refreshments, engaging in conversation, or simply daydreaming.

Decks are another popular amenity for rustic retreats. A generously sized deck offers the perfect location for hosting a festive summertime barbecue or soaking in the sun's rays. If you have the room, include an unpainted wooden picnic table for dining outdoors. As with any type of outdoor space, try to provide some sort of shelter from the sun, such as an awning.

Another idea is to have Adirondack chairs stationed in the yard. These durable yet comfortable furnishings will enhance the rustic style of your home and encourage relaxation. Or perhaps a hammock is more your speed. Whether you include one or all of these suggestions, you'll want to take full advantage of the setting around you.

# PICNIC TIME

*Apropos of your camplike surroundings, go on a picnic. Take advantage of your wonderful mountain locale or lakeside setting, and gather up all the right ingredients for a fun-filled outing. Here's a packing list to get you started.*

**A BLANKET.** Find one that you don't care about. It's very likely that this accessory will get grass-stained or muddy. You might want to select one that has a pattern and a number of colors so that any ground-in dirt may be camouflaged.

**TABLEWARE.** If you're bringing items other than finger foods, you'll need to be well equipped. If you desire a more elegant picnic, include silverware and perhaps your casual china; otherwise, use plastic and paper goods. Reusable plastic tableware may provide a sturdier choice than paper.

**STEMWARE.** Glasses are tricky—unless you're really out to impress, opt for plastic cups so that there's no chance of having to deal with broken glass. Today the options in plasticware are astounding—from colorful acrylic tumblers to high-style stemware.

**NAPKINS.** Have fun with these. Find green-and-white checked country-style dish towels, or for a more refined look, select napkins that are embroidered with a delicate design.

**SERVING ITEMS.** Create a feast for the eyes with the help of a few well-chosen accessories. Place fresh strawberries in a white basket, for instance. Employ different sizes of baking tins to serve vegetables; you could place baby carrots in one, celery in another, and cauliflower in a third for a variety of colors and shapes.

**ALL THE FIXINGS.** Create a meal fit for a king, and don't forget the condiments.

**FRESH FLOWERS.** Bring along a bouquet of flowers. You can keep them alive by wrapping the stems with wet paper towels and sealing in the moisture with a plastic bag secured by rubber bands. Cover the bottom with a piece of fabric—perhaps burlap for a rustic note—and tie it with ribbon or string.

**CANDLES.** You may need a citronella candle to ward off bugs if you are on an evening picnic. Another nice touch is a camping lantern.

# chapter six

# Whimsical

*H*AVE YOU EVER WALKED INTO A ROOM AND SIMPLY SMILED? YOUR DELIGHT MAY HAVE COME FROM WALLS THAT WERE

PAINTED IN AN UNUSUAL HUE, OR PERHAPS IT WAS THE COLLECTION OF ANTIQUE TOY TRAINS CAREFULLY MOUNTED IN LIEU OF

ARTWORK. IN ANY CASE, IT'S FUN TO ADD SOME WHIMSY TO YOUR HOME, AND THERE ARE COUNTLESS POSSIBILITIES FOR GIVING

YOUR COTTAGE A QUIRKY SENSE OF STYLE.

*page 134:* Give rooms a distinct personality with bursts of color. Here, regular flat bed sheets in boisterous hues revive chairs, resulting in a laid-back yet uniquely stylish look. An old-fashioned cupboard decked out in blue and yellow makes a worthy companion for the lively seating. *page 135:* A porch swing intro-duces an element of surprise into this traditional dining area. Surrounded by dark wood fur-nishings and walls, the novel piece stands out with its coat of green paint. *opposite:* Quirky touches abound in this cottage, which resembles something out of a fairy tale. From the offbeat chimney and undulating roof to the loglike balustrade, the dwelling engages the eye.

## *extraordinary exteriors*

Make the exterior of your cottage unique. Look to the work of internationally acclaimed architects, such as Frank Gehry, for inspiration. Although you may not want your home to have as much drama as the Guggenheim Museum in Bilbao, Spain, you can glean ideas about playing with scale and experimenting with materials.

One way to create whimsy is to do something unexpected. For example, why not make your front door oversized? Or include an odd-shaped chimney or a large outdoor fire-place in which you can actually set up a grill. A more subtle idea is to find decorative moldings that add unusual charm. And don't forget about paint. A splash of bright purple on the stair rail leading to your front door or a coat of turquoise blue around your windows is sure to catch the eye of onlookers.

Selecting interesting materials will also help achieve a whimsical look. Create a walkway from poured concrete, and infuse it with unusual objects along the way—imagine walking past starfish or seashells embedded in the flooring. Consider, too, mixing contrasting materials. For example, you could alternate between glass tiles and slate for your steps. Another idea is to mix wood and metal for your rail-ing. When doing something out of the ordinary, check with a building inspector or contractor to find out what is safe.

Don't forget to accessorize. Find a quirky flag that adds color to your exterior. Or give your cottage a name, and share it with the world by hanging a fanciful sign over your door. Flea markets are a good source for one-of-a-kind acces-sories. Peruse these treasure troves and look for fun-filled items. You might discover the perfect old-fashioned mailbox or an unusual door knocker.

*left:* Add whimsy on a small or large scale. A traditional home tends to benefit from just a few special features. Layers of trim, including wheellike inserts and colorful shutters around the front door, set this house apart from the others on the block.

*opposite:* The statuesque architecture of this home makes a strong statement. Even the wood fence zigs and zags to add visual interest.

*right:* Can't figure out what's right for your windows? Try this approach, and jazz up the view with a colorful painted border. The lively trim coordinates with the collection of Jadeite plates on display. *opposite:* What a floor show! The snazzy linoleum creates a retro mood and sets the stage for an assortment of brightly hued furnishings.

## *out of the box*

Once inside, the surprises can surround you. Think about the layout of your spaces. Can you create oddly shaped rooms? Or do you want to include winding hallways to achieve an Alice in Wonderland–like effect? You can also add a sense of drama and delight by playing with ceiling heights. For example, lower the ceiling at the entryway to signal the transition into your cottage, then raise the height of your living room. The contrast offers an unusual sensation.

Color provides a relatively easy way to take your decor up a notch. Bright colors can certainly inject a jaunty note.

Perhaps you'll decide to bathe your kitchen in a cheery yellow so that you feel like it's sunny all the time. Another option is to create a high-energy atmosphere with shiny hot pink wallpaper in your bedroom or a zebra-striped print in the dining room.

Don't be afraid to try different treatments within one space. For example, leave three of your dining room walls white, and paint the fourth one a warm red or sky blue. Consider incorporating a mural, perhaps a scene from a fairy tale for your dining room or an underwater environment for your bath.

# Quirky Touches

*You don't need to be extravagant to set a whimsical mood. Here are some simple, surefire ways to give your rooms personality.*

*opposite:* There are so many ways to infuse your living spaces with personal spirit. Collect objects from flea markets; search for interesting items during your travels; and look for pieces that simply make you smile. Here, everything from the dolls to the lamp to the toss pillows expresses a love for the islands.

**Welcome visitors.** Paint all your interior doors different colors. A warm yellow may lead you to the dining room, while a hot pink might be just what you want to greet visitors before they enter the guest bedroom.

**Button up.** Cover the area beneath a chair rail with buttons of different sizes and shapes to create a tactile effect in your den.

**Get framed.** Instead of a poster or painting, why not frame an everyday item like a subway map? It's inexpensive, and it will quickly become a conversation piece.

**Fake it.** Include trompe l'oeil effects to visually expand cramped spaces in your cottage.

**Get wild.** Add flair to rooms with animal prints. Try a zebra-striped shower curtain for your bath or a leopard pillow in your bedroom.

**Look up.** We often forget the ceiling when decorating. Tin ceilings offer a kitschy sophistication, while a tented room provides an air of mystery and even romance.

**Reflect your taste.** Consider using mirrors in unusual ways. For example, rather than having a single large mirror in a bath or an entryway, try to find a collection of antique mirrors to make your rooms sparkle.

**Jazz it up.** Are you a music lover? Consider including instruments to adorn spaces. A violin placed on a chair in the corner of your dining room may be just the sculptural touch you need in order to add elegance.

**Think big.** Play with scale. Try an oversize wing chair in the living room or a giant toothbrush as artwork in your bath.

**Seeing spots?** No one can resist the charm and whimsy of polka dots. Whether on upholstery or curtains, these jaunty adornments will add life to any space.

**Have a bright outlook.** Lighting fixtures can offer plenty of whimsy. Whether it's a sconce in the shape of grapes or a floor lamp whose base is a mermaid, the lighting you select can be more than just practical.

*right:* For the bedroom, consider establishing a theme. In this cleverly designed kids' room, everything speaks of summertime fun. A screened door recalls hours spent on the porch, while baseball caps hung on picket fence headboards speak of ballpark glories. The grassy green and sunny yellow striped bedding completes the look.

## good vibrations

Furnishings and accessories provide a world of opportunities for filling interiors with a sense of whimsy. One approach is to mix and match styles. Combining, say, an old-fashioned Aga stove with a stainless steel SubZero refrigerator will offer an unexpected duality in the kitchen. Or create an eclectic setting in your living room by mixing a dainty Victorian settee with an aluminum-topped coffee table on casters. You could also outfit a living area with a conservative selection of furnishings, but introduce one note of unpredictability—perhaps an old-fashioned lamppost stationed in one corner.

Indeed, using everyday objects in unusual ways is a sure-fire way of delighting family and friends. Jazz up a bedroom by replacing an ordinary closet door with an old screened door from a back porch. Or create an eye-catching coffee table by using four stacks of big art books as the legs and placing a square glass surface on top. Novel designs like this are sure to spark conversation.

Many people fill their cottages with spirit by choosing a theme. A baseball fanatic could pay tribute to his favorite sport with a chair designed in the shape of a catcher's mitt, a painted floor that mimics a baseball diamond, and ballpark

# THEME PARTIES

Whether you're celebrating a special occasion or just bringing the gang together, the fun increases when you set a theme. If you don't already have an idea in mind, let the decor of your cottage be your guide. For example, if you've incorporated pieces from the 1950s, consider hosting a sock hop. Have your guests dress up in poodle skirts and saddle shoes, and accessorize your home accordingly. Mount old records on a wall, or hang them from the ceiling using fishing wire. You may even look into renting an old-fashioned jukebox (unless you already own one). Finally, serve up such old-time favorites as milkshakes and root beer floats.

A party thrown to celebrate a holiday comes with a made-to-order theme. Valentine's Day can be a fun excuse for a fete. Spice up your dining table with bright red linens, and place plenty of red roses all around the cottage. To keep the focus on the blooms, place the flowers in clear containers. Let votive candles infuse your living room with romance. In the kitchen, use heart-shaped topiaries to brighten up counters. Treat your guests to delicious chocolates and heart-shaped sugar cookies.

You could also select a holiday that often goes overlooked. How about Flag Day? On June 14, decorate your home with the American flag, and give miniatures out as gifts to guests. Or why not plan your revelries for the longest day of the year? This will give you more time to enjoy your party. Take advantage of the sun's extended presence and make this an outdoor event.

Planning a theme party around an activity is another direction to take. Whether it's an Easter egg hunt, a painting party, or a cooking extravaganza, you can outfit your home to reflect the occasion. If you're hosting a cooking party, for instance, adorn your front door with a cheerful apron or an attractive serving piece—a large spoon hung on the front door is sure to set the mood. Also, find ceramic fruits or vegetables to accessorize the kitchen. Once your guests settle in, give them all chef's hats and aprons as a welcome to the party. For a personal touch, have these items embroidered or printed with the name of the party or some witty slogan pertaining to the event.

Yet another source of inspiration is the locale of your cottage. If your retreat is near the beach, consider a clambake. Put out blankets to sit on or set up tables and chairs, include tiki torches filled with citronella oil to ward off mosquitoes, and let guests enjoy their meal under the stars. Serve up a delicious feast of lobsters, clams, and corn on the cob—and don't forget some ice cream for dessert. You could use a whimsical object such as a child's sand bucket or a wheelbarrow as to hold food or supplies. The resulting party is sure to be a hit for guests of all ages.

*opposite:* A picket fence theme graces chairs and a wraparound bench, bringing a touch of amusement to meals. *right:* A charming setting, with furnishings dressed in white, gets a splash of pizzazz with a coat of yellow paint. The sunny hue sets the room aglow, while a chandelier sporting daisies injects a dash of whimsy.

*above:* Be creative when it comes to details and accessories. Reflecting the cottage's seaside location, this innovative floor treatment—featuring a painted starfish and sea foam—mimics the ocean lapping at the shore.

Perhaps you are drawn to rooms decorated in the Art Deco style, dating from the 1920s and 1930s. You might transform your bathroom by creating a bold, graphic pattern on your floor or tub surround. Or perhaps you'll come across the perfect rug with a strong geometric design—allow this dream find to take center stage in your living room. Keep in mind that during this period synthetics were all the rage, so don't overlook a chair upholstered in acrylic or a cabinet made from a plastic product such as Lucite. In the dining room, hang a sculptural chandelier that dates from the Art Deco period. For your bedroom, create a dressing area that includes a table with rounded corners and an oversize mirror.

Since cottages by nature have a diminutive scale, you may need only small touches to inject your spaces with whimsy. Folk-art accessories can make delightful additions. Place a whirligig on top of a hand-painted chest to spice up your living room, or set an iron horse on your dresser to wake up to every day.

memorabilia covering the walls. In a bedroom, a film buff might include a glamorous Hollywood-style dressing table, complete with bright lights and a director's chair, as well as old-fashioned movie posters featuring legendary stars.

If you prefer a lighter touch, there are more subdued ways of adding whimsy. For example, you could give family and friends a blast from the past by filling your spaces with retro pieces. Consider a midcentury-modern scheme for your living room, for instance. If you're a fan of *The Brady Bunch*, you'll know just what to do. You might include such features as shag carpeting, streamlined sofas and chairs, and modular furnishings. The colors in this room will most likely be muted—olive greens, eggplants, and burnt oranges are appropriate.

Other small touches include placing a pastel pink old-fashioned mixer on your kitchen countertop, or designating a special spot on the wall for a fun collection, such as an assortment of Pez dispensers. All you need is a few playful elements to give your interiors a quirky sense of style. Try things like beanbag chairs, a zigzag-edged window shade, or star-shaped toss pillows. What about adding tassels or pompoms to the bottom of a slipcovered chair? All of these options are sure to fill your cottage with a lighthearted, carefree spirit. Be creative: one entertaining idea is to paint a board game—perhaps a checkerboard—onto the floor of your bedroom. Whether you want to make a bold statement or a subtle one, bringing whimsy into your home allows for a bit of fun when decorating.

# Starting a Collection

If you've always admired your friends' interesting collections and the way in which they fill a home with personality, why not start your own? Where do you begin? First, determine where you'd like to put this collection. Since your cottage may be small, you may not want to start collecting Windsor chairs. If you're short on space, consider thinking on a smaller scale.

Next, look through magazines and visit flea markets. Are there particular items to which you're drawn? A collection is a very personal thing, so don't be swayed by what's trendy or what your neighbor likes. It has to be something that is special to you. Your decision might be determined by a family heirloom or a memory. Perhaps you often think about your grandmother's home-cooked meals. What type of dishes did she have? What about her silverware? Many silverware styles that have been discontinued can still be found at antiques stores or flea markets, as well as at live and Internet auctions.

Once you figure out what you like, do your research. Learn about the particular characteristics of these pieces. Also, try to get a sense of what they are worth. You certainly want to be knowledgeable when you've finally ready to buy. Here's a tip: always let the dealer give you a price first, then negotiate. The original number will serve as a point of reference. If you make the first offer, you won't have leverage if the dealer accepts too quickly, and you'll always wonder if you offered too much. Do, however, have a top price in mind. This will keep you from going over your budget, especially if you want to purchase more than one piece. And remember that a collection is something that develops over time, so don't rush into buying every piece of milk glass you can find. Take your time, and enjoy this pleasant pastime.

*below:* Displaying favorite collectibles allows you to share your interests with others. Here, a set of wall-mounted shelves showcases an assortment of beloved lady head vases.

*opposite:* A nautical theme makes bedtime fun for a child. The red, white, and blue palette takes its cue from a collection of life preservers employed as wall art. A small sailboat, a couple of miniature oars, and some ship paintings enhance the overall scheme. *right:* Since there isn't a window in this cottage bath, a trellis with a faux vine and votives provides outdoor ambience. (If you try something similar in your own space, make sure that none of the leaves are in danger of catching on fire.) When necessary, loose draperies can be pulled shut to give bathers privacy.

## *outdoor fun*

Enliven your yard, porch, or patio with a bit of whimsy, and you'll create an inviting setting to enjoy with family and friends. Maybe you'll uncover an unusual swing at a garage sale and install it on your front porch. Or you might outfit your yard with a table surrounded by chairs in an assortment of styles. A great way to do this is to visit a flea market and find a few chairs that are different but work well together. You can also paint the chairs in a variety of colors. Be sure to use paints made for outdoor furnishings, which are readily available at most home centers.

Design your outdoor area to mimic a storybook setting. Create narrow, winding paths, and hang signs on trees to intrigue visitors. Or purchase knee-high chess pieces and set them up on your front lawn. You could also try to find an outdoor sculpture that you'd like to see on a daily basis. While a Calder is beyond all but the most extravagant of budgets, you might seek out a local artist who designs fanciful mobiles. Perhaps you prefer a nonmoving piece, such as an iron rooster or a colorful welcome sign. On a simpler note, you could place a vintage red wagon on your lawn and fill it with a container garden of festive blooming plants. Any of these options are sure to provide guests with a memorable welcome.

Don't forget your driveway. There's no reason this utilitarian feature needs to be black or gray. Why not let your children paint their favorite designs on it? These will fade over time, but you can turn the painting of the driveway into an annual event. You might even make a party out of it and invite friends and neighbors to help.

A whimsical retreat is sure to offer many hours of delight. In fact, any cottage—from a peaceful sanctuary by the sea to a quaint escape in the countryside to a rustic hideaway in the mountains—will do the same. Remember that your cottage is a work in progress. So don't rush out and feel like you need to adorn every nook and cranny immediately; instead, take your time, enjoy the journey, and cherish all the memories that come along with it.

*opposite:* A table surrounds the trunk of an old tree, expanding the use of the backyard without sacrificing the tree's life. Painted chairs encourage folks to gather round. *above:* Bunches of roses and an old-fashioned sign enliven a corner of this cottage.

*left:* Pink trim, scrolled molding, and two rocking chairs give this Victorian home its charm. By having one chair painted white and the other in natural wood, the traditional symmetry of the cottage becomes pleasantly off balance. *opposite:* Filled to the brim with upbeat furnishings and accents, this deck is bound to lift spirits. Pastel hues contribute to the cheerful atmosphere, while a lamp shade decked out in buttons injects a whimsical note. Other eye-catching accessories include a birdcage, a vintage watering can, and an abundance of plants and flowers.

# Source Directory

## furnishings & accessories

Adirondack Country Store
252 North Main Street
P.O. Box 210
Northville, NY 12134
(518) 863-6056
www.adirondackcountrystore.com

Adirondack Store
109 Saranac Avenue
Lake Placid, NY 12946
(518) 523-2646
and
90 Main Street
New Canaan, CT 06840
(203) 972-0221

Beach Cottage Linens
225 Redfern Village
St. Simmons Island, GA 31522
(877) 451-6994
www.beachcottagelinens.com

Charles P. Rogers Brass & Iron Beds
55 West 17th Street
New York, NY 10011
(800) 272-7726
www.charlesprogers.com

Crate & Barrel
(800) 323-5461
www.crateandbarrel.com

Ficks Reed
Cincinnati, OH
(513) 985-0606
www.ficksreed.com
*Rattan and wicker furnishings*

French Country Living
(800) 485-1302
www.frenchcountryliving.com

Illuminations
(800) CANDLES
www.illuminations.com
*Candles and candle accessories*

L. & J.G. Stickley, Inc.
Stickley Drive
P.O. Box 480
Manlius, NY 13104
(315) 682-5500
www.stickley.com
*Arts and Crafts/Mission furnishings*

Laura Ashley Home Collection
www.laura-ashleyusa.com

Laura Fisher/Antique Quilts &
  Americana
1050 Second Avenue, Gallery #84A
New York, NY 10022
(212) 838-2596

Maine Cottage
Yarmouth, ME
(207) 846-1430
www.mainecottage.com

Martha by Mail
(800) 950-7130
www.marthabymail.com

Old Hickory Furniture Company
(800) 232-2275
*Rustic furniture*

Pier 1 Imports
(800) 44PIER1
www.pier1.com

Pierre Deux
(888) PIERRE-2
www.pierredeux.com
*French country furniture and
accessories*

Rejuvenation Lamp & Fixture Co.
(888) 401-1900
www.rejuvenation.com

Shabby Chic
Santa Monica, CA
(310) 394-1975
and
Chicago, IL
(312) 649-0080
www.shabbychic.com

Waverly
(800) 423-5881
www.waverly.com

## outdoor furnishings & fixtures

Country Casual
(800) 284-8325
www.countrycasual.com

Fran's Wicker & Rattan Furniture
(800) 531-1511
www.franswicker.com

Orvis
(800) 541-3541
www.orvis.com

Smith & Hawken
(800) 981-9888
www.smithandhawken.com

Vermont Outdoor Furniture
(800) 588-8834
www.vermontoutdoorfurniture.com

Vintage Woodworks
Quinlan, TX
(903) 356-2158
*Screen doors, porch doors, and
gingerbread trim*

Wicker Warehouse
(800) 989-4523
www.wickerwarehouse.com

Wood Classics
Gardiner, NY
(845) 255-7871
*Teak outdoor furnishings and
porch swings*

# Index

## *photo credits*

©Philip Beaurline: p. 139

©Grey Crawford/BeateWorks.com: p. 69

©Carlos Domenech: p. 84

Elizabeth Whiting & Associates/©Michael Dunn: pp. 37, 54; ©Di Lewis: p. 61

©Phillip Ennis: p. 12 (Architect: Armand Benedict)

©F & E Schmidt Photography: p. 65

©Michael Garland: p. 141

©Tria Giovan: pp. 27 top, 89

©Gross & Daley: pp. 5, 13 (Pi Gardiner house), 15 (Pi Gardiner house), 95 (Pi Gardiner house), 134, 135, 138, 144

©Kari Haavisto: pp. 20, 42, 56 left, 75, 97

©image/dennis krukowski: pp. 19, 83 (Designer: Francis Russell Design Decoration, Inc. New York, NY), 132–133 (Landscape Designer: Bruce John Davies, ASLA, PP; Designer/Homeowner: Judy Mashburn)

©Jessie Walker Associates: pp. 59 (Designer: Susan Chastain, Chicago), 66, 67, 107, 110, 117, 147

©Kit Latham: pp. 100–101

©Chris A. Little: p. 109

©Mark Lohman: pp. 6, 35, 44, 45, 47, 51, 56 right, 71, 74, 85, 104–105, 137, 143, 148, 149, 155

©Rob Melnychuk: p. 23

©Keith Scott Morton: pp. 21, 62, 105

©Bradley Olman: p. 140

Red Cover/©Brian Harrison: pp. 11 (Designer & homeowner: Binnie Hudson), 39, 40 (Designer & homeowner: Anthony Little of Osborne & Little), 68 (Designer: Binnie Hudson), 79, 92 (Designer & homeowner: Jean Hill), 150; ©Andrew Twort: p. 60 (Designer: David Mondel; Garden designer: Keith Anderson); ©Andreas von Einsiedel: p. 77 (Architect & Designer: Giles Vincent)

©Ivanthe Ruthvn: p. 27 bottom

©Samu Studios: pp. 18 (Courtesy Hearst Publications; Stylist: Margaret McNicholas), 26 (Courtesy Hearst Publications; Architect: Sam Scofield, A.I.A. 802-253-9948; Stylist: Margaret McNicholas), 32–33 (Courtesy Hearst Publications; Architect: Noelker Hull 717-263-8464; Stylist: Margaret McNicholas)

©Claudio Santini: p. 98 (Richard & Mollie Mulligan Sunset Cottage Antiques, Los Angeles, CA)

©Brad Simmons: pp. 43, 50, 73 (Architect: Stephen Dynia; Stylist: Joetta Maulden), 78, 80–81 (Designer: David Ross & Brent Waldock, David Ross Interior Designers; Stylist: Joetta Maulden), 86, 87 (Designer: Millie Huckabay, The Cottage at Crabapple, Alpharetta, GA), 96, 106, 111 (Log Manufacturer: Hiawatha Log Homes), 119 (Architect: Jonathan Foote), 122 (Designer: Delia Spradley), 124 (Builder: Back Country Builders; Stylist: Joetta Maulden), 125 (Log Manufacturer: Real Log Homes), 126 (Log Manufacturer: Appalachian Log Structures), 128 (Designer: Millie Huckabay, The Cottage at Crabapple, Alpharetta, GA), 129 (Architect: Don Briemhurst), 151

©Tim Street-Porter: pp. 36 (Designer: Rachel Ashwell), 48, 49 (Designer: Rachel Ashwell), 55 (Designer: Rachel Ashwell), 63 (Designer: Joe Ruggiero), 72

©Tim Street-Porter/BeateWorks.com: pp. 53 (Designer: Richard Sherman), 82 (Designer: Tom Callaway), 116 (Designer: Barbara Barry), 146

©Brian Vanden Brink: pp. 8 (Architect: Mark Hutker Associates), 16 (Architect: Mark Hutker Associates), 17 (Architect: Rob Whitten), 25 (Architect: Scholz & Barclay), 29 (Architect: Stephen Blatt), 30–31 (Architect: Bernhard & Priestly), 41, 57 (Architect: Quinn Evans), 90, 91 (Architect: Jane Doggett), 93 (Architect: Stephen Foote), 94, 108, 113 (Builder: Bullock & Company, Log Home Builders), 114 (Builder: Jack Sobon), 115 (Architect: Bernhard & Priestly), 118 (Builder: Bullock & Company, Log Home Builders), 120 (Architect: Peter Bohlin), 121 (Architect: Rob Whitten), 123 (Architect: Stephen Blatt), 127 (Architect: Stephen Blatt), 130 (Builder: Heartwood Log Homes), 131 (Builder: Bullock & Company, Log Home Builders), 152, 154

©Dominique Vorillon: pp. 2, 22, 24 (Designer: Gérard Faivre), 52, 58, 70, 76 (Designer: Stephen Schubel), 99, 102, 103, 153